girl*power*

girl*power*

TIME-TESTED SECRETS
FOR GETTING
WHAT YOU WANT FROM A MAN

Helen Austin, Julie Balloo, Sophie Davies,
Alison Goldie, Marian Pashley, Gina Ryan and Liz Webb

ORION
MEDIA

First published in 1997 by Orion Media
An imprint of Orion Books Ltd
Orion House
5 Upper St Martin's Lane
London WC2H 9EA

Copyright © Orion Books Ltd 1997

Designed and produced by
THE BRIDGEWATER BOOK COMPANY

All rights reserved. No part of this publication may be reproduced, stored in a retrieval system, or transmitted, in any form or by any means, electronic, mechanical, photocopying, recording or otherwise, without the prior permission of the copyright owner.

A CIP catalogue record for this book is available from the British Library.

ISBN 075281 0464

Repro by Pixel Colour Ltd
Printed and bound by Butler & Tanner Ltd,
Frome and London

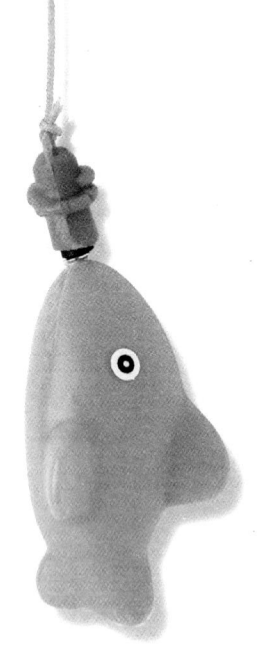

CONTENTS

Introduction 6
The rules of role-playing 8
Where to find true love 10
How to keep cool on the first date 12
Treat 'em mean keep 'em keen 14
Him meeting your friends you meeting his 16
How to play hard to get 18
When love is blind or protecting a stupid friend or little sister from falling for the wrong man 20
A guide to love potions 22
Dressing to impress .24
Making the most of sex manuals and videos 26
Romantic phone calls 28
Ways of letting him down gently 30
The rules of jealousy .32
Making up after breaking up 34
The rules of body language 36
Role models in love .38
A guide to love poems 40
Love and romance in novels 42
Love and romantic heroes 44
The do's and don'ts of office romance 46
The rules of divorce .48
Dealing with proposals of marriage 50
A guide to the top slushy films 52
How to have a bit on the side and get away with it 54
The truth about fairy-tale love 56
Finding love at the dating agency 58
A guide to plastic surgery 60
Leaving love notes 62
Advice on love and infatuation 64
Tips on love and seduction 66

History lessons in love 68
The do's and don'ts of love on your honeymoon 70
How to deal with love and hygiene or how important is the "H"-word in keeping love on the boil? 72
Love is full of surprises 74
First love never dies: how to deal with first love highs and first split blues 76
Mistaking love with friendship 78
A guide to lovey dovey presents 80
Love in the first few weeks of a relationship 82
A guide to romantic weekends 84
Facing up to the "C"-word 86
Confidential girlie chats 88
The rules on breaking up 90
How to make the first move 92
A guide to holiday romance 94
How to keep an interest in your lover's career 96
Valentine's cards 98
The high and lows of romance with the older man 100
Introducing him to mum and dad 102
The rules on moving in together 104
Advice for your wedding night 106
Romantic music to get you in the mood 108
Real together things to do 110
Acknowledgements .112

girl*power*

INTRODUCTION

GirlPOWER!

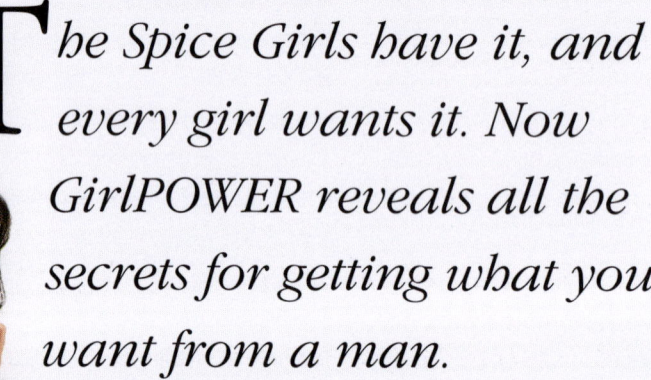

The Spice Girls have it, and every girl wants it. Now GirlPOWER reveals all the secrets for getting what you want from a man.

From thirteen to thirty it's the anthem of the year. Every girl instinctively knows some of the do's and don'ts for getting what she wants from a man. It used to be the man's territory to 'love them and leave them'. Now a huge team of street-wise girls have shared the wisdom of the ages and

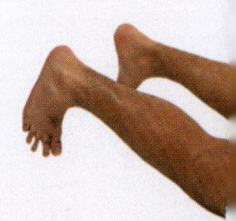

written GirlPOWER, the road map to ruling relationships for the 90s girl.

Start by learning from the great men-manipulators of history and move on to how to handle the randy little blighters on any and every occasion. How to find a man, from supermarkets and dating agencies to discos and blind dates. In easy stages we show how to remain in control.

Then there are the most important rules... those for the rest of your life... making him think he's in charge.

girl*power*

THE RULES OF
ROLE-PLAYING

The only rule that applies in this area is: "If it works, don't try to fix it." Most of the love games or fantasies we harbour are harmless, so should be shamelessly exploited. Shame only enters the equation if you are overheard playing Strict Nurse to his Naughty Medical Student. So, as the song should have gone, "Stand on your man . . . if he gets a kick out of it" . . . and put on those stilettos.

ROLE-PLAYING

When on the look-out for a man, there are certain roles you can play that are guaranteed to gain any man's attention. The only drawback is that someday he's got to get to know the real you. So, unless you really possess a little-girl lispy voice and a tendency to drop things, watch how far you take the "little girl lost". When he finds out that you also earn your living as a criminal lawyer, he might feel a little cheated.

A better approach is to use play-acting to take advantage of any situation or opportunity.

If you are crushed on the tube or the rush-hour train, and he looks interesting, make it clear that you feel faint . . . You won't be lying. Who doesn't feel nauseous after spending an hour with their face jammed into some stranger's armpit? If HE is even a little bit of a gentleman, he will find you a seat or, even better, a taxi. It's classic damsel in distress à la Jane Austen, but it has the advantage that you don't have to spend the rest of your life playing a helpless dependant. You have to remember that everything has its place. Trying the same "feak and weeble" act in the office when the phones get busy won't get you a promotion, or even a date, as no one likes a limp wrist as a colleague. The most advisable role to play at work is the "But, Miss Jones you're beautiful without your glasses and bun" transformation at the out-of-office drinks party. Some have been known to wear spectacles without prescription lenses just to be able to effect that stunning change. If you are tempted to do the same but are cursed with defective sight, be careful, you might end up stuck with whoever picks you up when you trip over them on the way to the loo, and they might have a defective face that you won't see . . . until Monday.

UNIFORMS

Every nice girl loves a sailor, or a policeman, a fireman, a soldier, a doctor . . . yawn, or not, if you are one of those nice or quite naughty, girls.

Of course, some uniforms are definitely not sexy. Think fast-food chains and traffic wardens, but there are few girls who can resist a longing look at a passing fire engine. It's almost worth getting stuck up a tree.

Some women are uniform obsessed, it's the authority thing (says Freud). But it's difficult to take seriously those who try to claim that the swimming trunks on the pool attendant also count. Unfortunately, we all know someone who is a veritable ambulance chaser, who will bundle anyone who so much as looks a bit peaky into the back of an ambulance and be off with them to hospital. It's then all a bit embarrassing when the life-threatening cramps turn out to be mere indigestion, but at least the obsessed one has managed a longing gaze at a stethoscope and a white coat. If this is your thing, then take our advice – the best way to date a doctor is to go to university and study medicine, but if A-levels are not on your CV, next best is to get a job in the pub nearest to the local hospital. All doctors love their drink . . . really LOVE it. This approach will be "kill or cure", as watching the ninetieth inebriated houseman sing "Lily The Pink" whilst dropping his trousers will send you either into paroxysms of lust (if you are incurable) or screaming into the arms of the nearest dustman (if you are sensible).

There's the rub – the fantasy is generally much preferable to the reality. Any woman who has married a soldier will tell you how he comes home and tries to run the home like a barracks. All very well, but try getting a toddler to salute daddy. Dating a handsome policeman is lovely, unless you wish to keep your friends. Just about everyone comes over as a bit guilty, about something real or imagined, the moment they are in the company of one of Her Majesty's finest. It's just not conducive to a good night out. If you think that sounds bad, try introducing your friends to Special Branch – perfectly sane people start behaving like they've murdered their granny and stashed her away in the boot of their car when the worst thing they've ever done in their life is park on a double yellow line.

Unless you have a cast iron will and the patience of Florence Nightingale, best keep it all strictly to fantasy, which leads us on to . . .

DRESSING UP

The art of dressing up can combine both uniforms and role-playing to devastating effect. It's best to go out with a clay-footed accounts clerk and get him to dress up at the weekends. If he feels a little shy, or you feel silly suggesting it outright, get into it by going to a fancy-dress party. Make him wear whatever turns you on, and go over the top yourself. The erotic impact of your French maid's outfit will not be lost on him, particularly if he's done up as the Lord of the Manor, complete with riding crop and boots.

The fantasy enactment doesn't have to be that extreme, however.

Most men have some little weakness. Play to it. If he's a "leg man" wear seamed stockings to the pub one night – he'll lose at darts. If he likes his women voluptuous, invest in clever underwear, and take him out to dinner. The combined effect on his senses of good food, fine wine and a great cleavage will have you putting the classic *9½ Weeks* to shame.

Films are often useful guides. His favourite films are usually foolproof clues to his steamiest imaginings. If he likes *The Graduate,* play Mrs Robinson. If he's a fan of old movies, dress up like Marilyn Monroe and treat him like he's your sugar daddy. He'll soon get the idea.

girl*power*

WHERE TO FIND TRUE LOVE

According to official statistics, the workplace is supposed to be where most people find the "love of their lives" (and their embarrassing mistakes!). But if you spend your day behind the make-up counter at Boots, serving only women and guilty husbands (because perfume is a bigger sorry than flowers) or in a tiny office where there's only the spotty gopher and forgetful Mr Pace who's been off the list ever since he got his false teeth, you need more than a little help from Cupid – you're more likely to need a bloody miracle.

These are, however, some other places where you may be lucky in love...

IN PUBS AND CLUBS

Okay for a fling, but if you're after the real thing, call a cab. For a start, drink is involved. A girl's eyesight deteriorates in direct proportion to the amount of dry white wine she consumes. The Tom Cruise look-alike you arrange to meet on Saturday turns out, under the cold lights of shopping city, to look more like Curly Watts. If by some miracle he really is attractive and interesting, then chances are he's a love cheat and he's doing the dirty on his live-in girlfriend. Tell-tale signs: he only tells you his first name, is vague about where he lives, and he takes your number but can't remember his own.

Some get blasé with success and may try to pass off the female voice that answers their phone as their mother. When that voice asks who the bloody hell you are the second time you ring, you shouldn't believe the excuse . . . "mother's got a little drink problem . . ."

When you get to this stage in your quest for true love it's time to try real life.

IN THE SUPERMARKET

The trolley pick-up is becoming a cliché, but it's a truth that all single men have to buy food that isn't curry or take-out pizza . . . eventually. Unless he really does still live with his mum and in that case, who's interested?

Look for a truly chaotic basket, they rarely have a trolley, the sort of basket whose contents make you feel slightly nauseous. Chocolate milk nestling in to a smelly French cheese all being squashed by a designer cider? SINGLE BOY. Don't ever look aghast or say anything critical, men are extremely protective of their disgusting childlike comfort foods. Instead, ask him if he's tried the latest yukkie kiddies' breakfast cereal. How does it compare to Coco pops? Once you mention a liking for the forbidden milk-staining tooth-rotters he'll be smitten. Crunchy Coco fantasies will be racing through his mind and you'll be in them.

If you are pursuing true love in the supermarket it's best to keep away from the freezer aisle. The cold makes your nose go red, not pretty under striplights and there's something deeply unsexy about all those bags of super value food produced for mums trying to feed a family of ten on a budget. This might send you scuttling straight for the wines and spirits section with a trolley (or two).

ON THE BUS

However cute he may look, chances are he's poor, a tourist or banned from driving. None of these are particularly appealing propositions unless you want to be someone's holiday romance or get involved with some dodgy geezer who can't keep his car on the road.

One way to sort out the princes from the paupers is to pretend you're 20p short of your fare. If there are any solvent charmers lurking behind the newspapers, that will be their cue to help you out. Failing that, the bus driver might take pity on you and some of them are hot. Try the earring count. The more earrings crammed into one ear the better – this is his way of saying that he's wearing his uniform with ironic detachment. But let's face it girls – he's still a man in uniform.

AT CHURCH

This can mean anything in terms of social opportunity, depending on your religion or lack of it. It can mean a regular Sunday event with a bit of bell-ringing thrown in, even weekend jaunts away (of a strictly spiritual nature, though many Christians are not averse to the odd tipple to get over their inhibitions) and many people meet their spouse through the church. A case of God as matchmaker, or "It's Raining Men" for the girl who's prepared to look in the right places. To the rest of us, however, church visits consist of weddings, funerals, christenings and midnight mass on Christmas Eve. These are all (with the usual exception of funerals) a chance to meet men outside of your usual catchment.

At weddings the love train is already at full steam, all you need do is get on board. The men unwittingly look their best and, like lambs throwing themselves on to the butcher's slab, they walk into the most hard-sell monogamy convention of their lives. Relatives and friends become frenzied in their attempts to fix up singles and within minutes you will know the romantic status and profession of every single man in the room. Heaven help you if you are already attached but foolishly decide to leave your loved one at home, you'll probably get sent home with a spare.

Christenings offer a similar opportunity, although here there's more chance of being hit on by slimy older men who feel neglected. "Here, give us a kiss, it's okay, the wife's upstairs feeding the baby." – Yuck.

Invariably, the place will be swarming with children, which is a great way to suss the character of your object of desire. There is nothing quite so appealing as a man who is good with kids, especially overexcited kids who are full of cake and the dregs of abandoned champagne glasses. The man in question will be nothing less than a saint; do not let him leave without your phone number tattooed on his forehead.

girl*power*

HOW TO KEEP COOL on the first date

First dates are horrible. For a start you spend weeks, months or even years infatuated with some hunk. This is the sort of infatuation that he is so oblivious to that he treats you like his kid sister, but that is so obvious to everyone else that even his dog acts jealous around you. Then one day it happens. You stumble out of your front door looking like a bag lady, with a spot on your forehead that causes people in queues to let you go first, bump straight into him, whereupon he sees you for the first time as a woman and asks you out.

The first date will be horrific, partly due to nerves and partly because that is the law. If you enjoy a first date you are either blessed with a breathtaking lack of sensitivity (do you really think he's having a good time?) or you are only going out with him for a bet.

THE VENUE

If he's asked you, this is generally his decision. Where he takes you says a lot about him and can help you prepare so that you don't make a complete fool of yourself. The guy who says, "Hey babe, I'll pick you up at eight and we'll do something nice" is a sadistic pig. You'll put on high heels and a little black dress only to end up tottering around a funfair up to your ears in mud, trying not to look like Lady Di at a car-boot sale.

Most men are more specific and usually pick a restaurant, bar or cinema. Restaurants sound great, but are fraught with danger. Try not to eat anything other than mashed potato and blancmange because anything else will end up in your hair (spaghetti), in your lap (soup) or in your teeth (any green vegetable). If you do try ordering only mashed potato and blancmange, however, you'll come across as a crank or pregnant – neither of which is going to lead to a meaningful relationship, let alone a second date.

If it has to be a meal, take precautions. A toothbrush, plenty of tissues and a change of clothes. Don't forget to take plenty of money. That way you can throw down your half of the bill, run out of his life and into a cab the moment he utters the words, "But ever since my girlfriend left me, whenever I eat liver I like to imagine it's hers . . ."

Going to a bar is much easier, so long as you don't drink so much you forget your own name and so long as he doesn't drink so much that he forgets it too. This environment is one in which you can find out quite a lot about him. Is he generous? Is he a snob? Does he like to start fights?

The best place to go on a first date is the cinema. You can sit in the dark for most of the evening. After all, a first date resembles nothing so much as a job interview (except no one's sure who is the boss) so being saved too much visual scrutiny is a blessing.

It's the same debate as you try to leave the house. People say always wear your second-best clothes to an interview, be comfortable but smart – but if only it were so easy when making a first impression on HIM. So it's between the short skirt – too obvious? Or the jeans – too casual, and will they make me look fat? Perhaps a sack with a nice string at the neck. . .

One crucial decision for the first date is footwear. We've all seen it, a girl who is dressed to kill and looks fabulous, then as soon as she tries to move, she walks like a man in drag who's been lying about his shoe size. Never go for over-high heels or brand-new shoes on a first date and anyway, you might want to be able to walk really quickly when he suggests the foreign film with the words: "No really, it's very artistic." Then you spot the triple X rating in the tasteful blue lighting of the foyer, where everybody else queuing for their tickets are dodgy-looking old men all wearing a certain type of soiled raincoat and smelling of cheese.

HER
LOUD ENOUGH TO BE OVERHEARD
"You see I've got to the age now where I can't be bothered with time-wasters, I'm looking for someone who can commit to a relationship, that's why I put the ad in the paper."

HIM
"Is that the time? I'm not up to these late nights, I'll see you around."

CONVERSATION

Your kind old granny would never discuss religion or politics at a social gathering, but she should also have said, "Don't tell the chicken it's going to be dinner, until you've got a grip on its neck" or, in other words, leave all the discussions about exes and how many children you want until you've signed the pre-nuptial agreement. Nobody likes to feel that they are being judged and compared, so keep the conversation on topics such as religion and politics and what's in your CD collection.

If he starts telling you all about his ex-girlfriend or wife, be very wary. If he says it's all amicable and no hard feelings then he's either an emotionless robot or about to get back with her. You'll be remembered as the girl who helped him realize what a mistake he'd made (cheers!). If he rants on about what a bitch she was and how she never gave his mother enough respect then he's either a psycho or in the Mafia. Change your phone number and your name and move house.

LOVE AT FIRST SIGHT

Sometimes this happens. You meet someone and you know immediately that they think you're wonderful and you think he makes Brad Pitt look a bit ropey and Einstein a bit thick. Don't bother with all the nerve-wracking dating business, you know you're soul mates, use your time more effectively. Skip dinner, go straight to John Lewis and choose your wedding gifts.

girl*power*

Treat'em MEAN
Keep'em KEEN

Nobody ever fell in love with someone because they were nice. It doesn't even happen in fairy-tales. Good, yes. But not nice. We are not, however, recommending that you become known for kicking cute domesticated animals (unless it's the type that watches too much football). Think Madonna, not Cruella de Ville.

Man is, by nature, a lazy creature. Having grown up attended to by a mother who offers uncritical devotion. If he gets the same unquestioning adoration from you, he will think he need only give the same crumbs of sustenance to you that he does to his dear old mum, i.e. a phone call once a week and a set of matching toiletries (courtesy of Woolworths) each birthday and Christmas. Don't worry, it's not cruel – the thrill of the unexpected will keep him enthralled, as well as the occasional slap (verbal of course).

Just think – if only his mother had left him to make his own tea or iron his own shorts just a couple of times, how much easier your life would be.

If you're still not convinced you're quite up to it – here's some help.

TEN WAYS TO KEEP THE UPPER HAND

1 Buy an answerphone. Screen all of your calls. Even if you are in every day, all day, do not answer the phone. He will never be quite sure what you are doing or where you are. When he leaves a message, answer only every other one. When he asks when it's best to call or when you expect to be home, remember to be in, but don't pick up that phone. He will become so frustrated he will ask you to move in with him, just to convince himself that you are not a figment of his imagination.

2 Never tell him anything about your ex-boyfriends. The mystery will be unbearable. You are a woman of the world, so there were others, but if he gets to know anything about them he can turn this information to his advantage. If you say your ex was a bastard, he will paint himself as your shining knight. If you say he was kind and generous, he will decide he was a wimp and that he is the first real man you have ever had (i.e. one that is unkind and mean). It's best to simply go quiet and misty-eyed whenever the subject of ex-lovers is mentioned, and this tragic dignity will imply that, but for some cruel twist of fate, you would still be united with your one true love. As it is, you will make do.

3 Forget his name.

girl*power*

4 Forget how much sugar he takes in his tea. When he acts offended, apologize, and say, "I'm sorry, I just wasn't thinking…of YOU".

5 Introduce him to people as your current boyfriend. Or, even when you got engaged, refer to him only as your "friend". The implication is always that although you may go out with him and bring him to meet your family, you still regard yourself as an independent spirit. Or, in other words, as he will be given to understand, although you may have agreed to marry him, you are still open to offers, so he'd better show some respect and adoration at all times.

6 Use a favourite boys' trick against him. We've all heard the old line, "I'm so confused, I need some space . . ." at which point the girl feels like she must be some clinging, dull nag and resolves never to ask him to do the washing-up ever again. When he dares to ask you where you went with your mates last Friday night, as you had to stay in bed all Saturday with "a bit of a head", reply that he is not your keeper and that you feel hemmed in. Spend a couple of weeks having some "space" yourself and with any luck, in future, he will happily drive you to your nights out and even agree to pick you up if you ask, without ever a reproachful word.

7 Make sure that he knows how lucky he is to have you. If you don't actually have an infatuated admirer hanging around waiting for you to become available, make one up. Send yourself Valentine's cards and birthday trinkets (you can always keep the receipt and return them once the birthday is over); their job is done once you have been observed opening the beautifully wrapped parcel and exclaiming in delight and surprise: "Oh, look! But he really shouldn't have!"

8 When in a new relationship, don't see him more than a couple of times a week and make sure you cancel a few dates at short notice. He will soon get a picture of where he is in your list of priorities, that is second from bottom, just above dental-flossing, and will strive to do better.

9 If you do agree to move in together, never do his washing. Once every week or so, give him a fiver and send him out to the cinema while you have your mates over. When he has his mates round to watch the football, go out or simply disappear. Never do the "little woman" act of making snacks and fetching beers, you may as well change your name to Fido and carry his slippers in your mouth.

10 Never EVER say sorry. Even if you have crashed his car into a tree after having run down his whole family, all you need say is "Oh dear, that was a bit careless of me, still, we all make mistakes."

girl*power*

HIM MEETING YOUR FRIENDS
YOU MEETING HIS

So, you've been seeing each other for a few weeks in the blessed privacy of cinemas, out-of-the-way restaurants and his place. You both know that this is likely to be serious and you can tell he's gearing up to the "L" word, because he keeps paying you compliments and then stopping mid-sentence and acting all shifty, like a naughty schoolboy working up to a confession. In moments when he's been asleep you've rooted through his flat and are satisfied that he has no gun collection or torture chamber (not that you're paranoid). The next stage inexorably approaches, he has to be slotted into your life, filling those gaps that before were spent at evening classes in useless subjects that only single or unhappily married people join. This means he has to meet your friends.

HIM MEETING YOUR FRIENDS
THINGS NOT TO SAY

"Hi, I'd like you to meet Jonathan, he hasn't got any disgusting personal habits..."

1

What you are trying to do here is overcompensate for the fact that you know all your friends are looking for signs of some grotesque weirdness in him as we all, through our dating mishaps, gain a track record with our mates that becomes a kind of myth. "Oh you know Sharon," they say to each other, "she only dates cranks."

"Hi this is Jonathan, he's got a thing about women's shoes."

2

Okay, you're saying to your friends, I know you all think I only ever go out with cranks, but this guy's only got one little hang-up and actually I think it's quite endearing and harmless compared with the last one. They will think he's a pervert and he will be so embarrassed he will scrub your name from his address book. Some things are private; as Ricki Lake would say – you can share too much.

girl*power*

3 *"Hi, meet my future husband."*

Oh dear, don't you sound desperate, when all you are really trying to do in your clumsy way is let your friends know that this one is serious and no telling him hilarious stories of all my millions of exes please. However, your boyfriend now thinks that you are some kind of *Fatal Attraction* fan and that he'd better go home and start packing so that his family will find it easier to tidy up after the funeral.

At the end of the day you have to accept the reality that only after you've been happily married for forty years will your friends accept that your partner is perhaps right for you, though you could have done better, they will still say whenever you have a row over your grandchildren's manners. That's what friends are for. After all, if you do split up after six months you will expect them to be on your side and to cut him dead in the street, even if he's the one that's been dumped.

YOU MEETING HIS FRIENDS
WHAT NOT TO SAY:

1 *"Hi, mine's a pint of lager and a packet of crisps please. Anyone up for a curry later?"*

Oh dear, you might go out with your brother's rugby mates and arm-wrestle with the best of them, but with his friends you will never be anything but "her indoors" who gets in the way of the lads' night out. You will be viewed with suspicion if you try the "I'm one of the lads" tack; they won't believe it because, from now on, you are the enemy, so you might as well order a sweet white wine and get used to being patronized about football.

2 *"Hello, my darling Honeybuns has told me all about you."*

The baby talk is fine when you are alone. In public it will make him so embarrassed he will never be soppy with you ever again. To his mates it will sound like a declaration of war. "Look," you are saying, "I have turned him into my very own dancing bear, when I say jump, he leaves you at nine-thirty without even shelling out for his round."

3 *"Hi, so which one of you is it who's still a virgin . . .?"* (joke)

He will have shared secrets with you – things about his friends and family, because men are basically gossips as much as women. They just like to pretend that they are above that kind of female trivia. He might pretend it isn't the nasty, scurrilous half-truths of gossip, but that's exactly what it is, and should be treated with the respect it deserves. Memorize and store the information without breathing a word. His mate's secret virginity is no joke and is a fact that could be used against him, as a silencing tool, if he cuts up rough when it looks like you might be planning to marry his precious pulling-pal.

There is a best and a worst case scenario to be gained from all this suffering. At best, one or two of his mates might prove human enough to introduce to one of your single girlfriends. At worst, if he dumps you, you can always get revenge in the pointless and spiteful act of copping off with the most geeky of his mates, in front of him and everyone else, and then having the rumour put about that, surprisingly, geek-man is a far better lover than your most recent ex.

girl*power*

HOW TO PLAY HARD TO GET

A bizarre accident of genetics has resulted in the phenomenon whereby the male of the species values most those things that are the most difficult to achieve. Think of mountain climbing or flying to the moon. Of course, there are some women who indulge in these demanding but essentially futile activities and they are the sort who fall in love with celibate priests. Probably.

Playing hard to get is simply the logical manipulation of this masculine frailty. The most important word to remember is "playing". If you really are that hard to get he'll never have the initiative to find you. Men being the simple, unimaginative creatures that they are, the trick is to let them think they've climbed the metaphorical glass mountain to win your hand.

HOOKING YOUR FISH

There is a myth that if you stay at home knitting and being kind, one day a knight on a white charger will knock on your door and ask you to go bowling, leading eventually to a life of wedded bliss and even more knitting. WRONG.

You have to go out there and find Mr Right (trying out Mr Complete Bastard and Mr Fun-but-Unreliable on the way) but at the same time lead him to believe that he was doing the searching.

Remember Cinderella's lost glass shoe on the stair? Clever Prince Charming? That was no accident. Clever Cinders. She might as well have put a ring through his nose and called him Porky. She had him domesticated the minute she tripped down those steps. The mystery, the adventure . . .

THE SUCKER

Follow her example, it's an old trick. If you meet him at a party at his house, leave something behind. You'll have to get his number and call round for it, or better still, he'll have to deliver it to you. After all, you are just so busy, busy, busy, you don't know when you'll have time to pop by.

If you meet at a club, borrow his jacket when he's helping you to hail a cab and in your rush to jump in, forget to give it back. "I'm so sorry about that, cab drivers are very impatient and I must have been a tiny bit tipsy . . ."

Always remember, slightly tipsy is attractive, drunk as a skunk is about as attractive as its smelly namesake. By your fourth dry white wine you'll tell him the funny story about how you lost your virginity and on your fifth how much you still love your ex even though he is a complete bastard. Oh dear.

girl*power*

REELING HIM IN

This is the tricky bit. Once you are regularly dating, be frugal with your affections. Don't fall into bed on the first night. A good aid to restraint is to wear your most embarrassingly grubby, old, worn-out underwear for the first couple of weeks you are together. The necessity to prevent him even so much as glimpsing a hint of frayed and grey bra-strap will make you a veritable Sandra Dee in his presence and will sustain the mystery. (If he can't be bothered to play the game and gets stroppy, he has no long-term potential and should be thrown back.) Snogging is good, you want him to know you don't just see him as a brother and if he can't kiss he probably isn't good for much else – introduce him to your least best friend.

Let him ring you most of the time and when he suggests a date, turn down the first evening he can make. It will be clear that you are more in demand than he is. He will be intrigued, you must have a very full and interesting life if you aren't prepared to drop everything to go out with him. After all, every man thinks that he is the centre of his universe and he will become curious about your life. This sensation will make him a little nauseous at first, thinking of others is not a natural male habit, but once he gets used to it, this curiosity will serve only to increase his infatuation and wonder. Your rating on the interest scale will be roughly equivalent to a caveman seeing his first fire. Keep it stoked.

HIS LAST GASP

Never be the first one to say "I love you". When he first says it to you, laugh in his face. We know this sounds harsh; it is harsh, but it works. In his mind, you, being a girl, will be waiting and hoping for his ultimate approval and those three little words are it. It's the male idea of a trump card. Say the "L" word, they tell each other in pubs, and you need never take her out again. "She will be so grateful, she will massage your feet whilst you watch the footie," they promise. When the girl in question reacts with a snort of derision and concern for his mental health you can be sure he will never say it again until he really means it. When that time comes it will be accompanied by the keys to his flat or a ring with a shiny bit.

WHEN LOVE IS BLIND
OR PROTECTING A STUPID FRIEND OR LITTLE SISTER FROM FALLING FOR THE WRONG MAN

As someone once said, "no man is perfect, but some men are scum." Unfortunately it always seems to be your sweet and trusting younger sister or naïve friend who paid most attention in nursery school when they told the story about the frog prince. They were obviously off sick for the story of the big, ugly troll who lies in wait under the bridge near the pond with the lily pads, pretending to be a frog, just in case some poor girl took the wrong turning at the sign pointing East to fairyland and West to nightmare.

If you are lucky enough to be a member of a family with Mafia connections, you know how to handle these things. If you happen to be one of those normal law-abiding saps like the rest of us, the problem can end up related to you and you are faced with a lifetime of the troll turning up at every family occasion until death grants you a blessed release.

As they say, love is blind, but best mates and older sisters are not. It is up to you to give the appropriate advice and guidance to help her steer a safe course and, when that fails, pay someone to frighten the life and lust out of him.

TYPES OF SCUM

1. THE SERIAL BASTARD

He's the sort who is very charming and attentive when he is first attracted to a girl, but as soon as he becomes sure he has her heart or virginity (depending on his hang-ups and her age) he will dump her. If by some strange chance he ends up living with her or married to her, he will spend all his time undermining her self-esteem. He is usually quite attractive so can easily leech on to some nice innocent girl, but will show signs early on, if you are prepared to notice them. All his exes will no longer even speak to him, he will talk about women as slags/bitches (even his own mother) and he will HATE you. If you cannot persuade her to see sense then the only sure way to shake him off is to...

a) sidle up to him early on and tell him that she's planning to have his babies

OR

b) introduce him to a girl who is richer or more attractive than your friend/sister (it may hurt her at first but she will get over it).

2. THE MARRIED MAN

He's older, more experienced and better off than all the boys she has gone out with so far. He is a MAN not a boy, plus all the excitement of the secret meetings can be very addictive. The downside is that not only can he never be trusted an inch, if he can cheat on his family, then why not his girlfriend, but also that being a mistress is tacky and ultimately lonely. He will never leave his wife because it's not really "love" for him but a game; he only really loves the secrecy and the glamour of a younger woman. The quickest way to stop her falling for this one is to wait until she's gone to the Ladies and then tell him that it's such a small world, not only are you his girlfriend's sister but also a very good friend of his wife.

THE OCTOPUS

We've all been there, the drinks in the pub to meet her new boyfriend. He seems quite human and then as soon as her back is turned he's got his hand on your knee and you realize that you were wrong. He's not human after all and in terms of evolution he's somewhere below a goldfish. Stab him through the hand with a fork and when he yelps in pain say very loudly: "I'm sorry, was that you touching me up? I thought it was some sexually inadequate needle-dick who couldn't keep a single woman satisfied, never mind two."

THE DODGY GEEZER

This guy is attractive, particularly to the naïve, overprotected type of girl. He seems to be so streetwise and charming in a rough diamond kind of way. He will also be very generous when things are going well ("If you know what I mean darlin', had a bit of good luck . . .") and try to borrow a tenner off you when things are tight. When asked what his line of work is, he will laugh long and hard at the W-word and utter the immortal, "this and that, you know how it is", or more worrying "I'm in the family business". The reasons for going out with her will be twofold. She makes him look good to his dodgy associates, his trophy girlfriend (remember the Kray twins' affection for pert blonde starlets?) and her respectability and trusting nature will provide him with alibis when needed. Best approach with this one is to start going out with a policeman and suggest a double date. That will be the last you will see of him, well, that is until you next turn on *Crimewatch*.

THE SLOB

"Course I love ya, I ordered you a pizza didn't I?" Uncharming as this man is, he still manages to get a girlfriend. One who's just been let out of a convent perhaps, or been released from prison and is a little bit desperate?

No, quite normal women happen to suffer from the misapprehension that they can change him. Well, they say, if he can get out of bed to get to the footie, then maybe one day he could get up for work. WRONG. His idea of making an effort is to wear a shirt that only has food down it, rather than vomit. His idea of romance is ringing you from his bed when you are at work to ask you to pick up something special for tea on your way home, oh, and maybe a video? Something violent? His idea of a perfect woman is one who acts just like one of his boozy mates down the pub, but then manages to be sober enough to cook him a fry-up when you get in after midnight, and gets up to go to work in a good mood after making him a cooked breakfast.

He must be dispatched with, and quick. Offer him a job, any job, it doesn't have to be a real one because he's never going to turn up for work. With all his excuses for his laziness blown away, the scales should fall from her eyes. He really is just an idle pig and he will grow trotters and a curly tail as she watches in despair.

girl*power*

A GUIDE TO
LOVE POTIONS

Oh, it sounds so simple put like that – a pill you can just slip into his coffee to get him going – although since the turn of the century patent products have promised just that. Who could forget "Zip", "Passionette" and best of all "Stifferene". Nowadays there are aphrodisiacs such as Sex-O-vit – but why not just PhOOOOOOOOOr! Anyway if the truth be known – they're just vitamins and minerals (although these will definitely perk men up, given their usual diet of cereal and chips), or genital irritants and diuretics which focus attention on the sexual parts – like most blokes need help to focus there!

However, the following love potions do have some drawbacks:

- **Damiana:** small Mexican shrub – bitter taste.
- **Spanish Fly:** crushed cantharis vesicatoria beetle – irritation takes absolutely ages to subside.
- **Ohimbe:** West African tropical tree – causes nausea.
- **Strychnine:** decidedly lethal in larger doses.

Remember these products for an overdose when you get sick of your lover, but until then, forget them and plan this special aphrodisiac night for him.

But do remember, sexual desire is: **part physical** as in health (but you can have great passion with pneumonia, a broken collar bone and no food or sleep when inspired **part mental** due to symbolism (but hard to predict – like the man who famously could only get an erection standing in a bath of cold spaghetti) **part loony-tunes-who-knows-why.** *

RECOMMENDED POTIONS
BREW UP A SPELL

- Desiccated testicles of any animal – the Romans chose wild randy ones like a wolf or deer so a football supporter's will do.
- Heart of toad and dead man's fat. The Church of the Middle Ages forced guilt, sin and evil to be linked with sex – alternatively all of these can also be quite a turn on: cheating, sleeping with best friend's boyfriend or your boyfriend's father – in your parents' bed.
- Rhino horn and ginseng root – due to the phallic shape, so you could just use powdered ruler (all depends how well stocked your local Tescos is).

PREPARE A 1000-YEAR-OLD LOVE DRINK
Ingredients
7 coriander seeds, cup of water
Method
Grind the coriander seeds together while naming the loved one, add the cup of water and dissolve the seeds while chanting "warm seed, warm heart, never let them be apart".

*But remember the loony-tunes-who-knows-why element and include lots of the most important ingredient: MUTUAL ENTHUSIASM IN THE FIRST PLACE.

girl power

OR...

The more modern version involving two bottles of cheap white wine and chanting, while in floods of tears "please God, don't let me be alone and unloved and die a spinster".

PREPARE YOURSELF WITH SOME ANCIENT REMEDIES

BATHE IN CHESTNUT BLOSSOM SCENT

Recommended in the 18th Century by the Marquis de Sade – probably because the flowers have the same chemical make up and smell of sperm – no wonder "things happen after a Badedas bath". It seems that some men sprinkle their bedsheets with chestnut blossom.

SCENT YOURSELF WITH

- The perfumes civet and musk – pungent secretions from glands at the rear of the cat-like civet and musk deer – so alternatively get your cat to sit on your lap and fart a bit.
- Human pheromones taken from the hair follicles of the underarm and groin (i.e. personal sweat, banned in perfumes in the USA – surprising for such an erotic race).

CHEW SOME CARAWAY SEEDS

To scent your breath – mythical turn-on properties for men, probably because the seeds promote lactation in nursing mothers and blokes are into that kind of thing – but only because it covers bad breath, so sugar-free gum should also do the trick.

INSTEAD OF EYE-SHADOW

Use soot from inside a burnt skull – Indians used skulls from funeral pyres but you're bound to have an ex-boyfriend's lying around the place somewhere.

WEAR CHARMS

Rhino horn, seeds, nuts, ears of corn, garter, stockings, Wonderbra... or just wear less.

WHEN HE ARRIVES

CRACK A FEW JOKES

Humour is considered a great turn-on, e.g. "What do you call a man without an erection? You don't call him."

BE CRUEL

A well-known aphrodisiac. The Romans had a circus of cruelty called the Circus Maximus ringed with brothels to be visited after several adrenalin rushes – so tell him he looks shit and scratch him a bit.

PRESS-UPS FOR BOTH OF YOU

Beta endorphins in the blood enhance a feeling of happiness.

SMOKE SOME HEMP

Which will relax you – but be warned, while it removes inhibitions it can intensify any feelings of sexual inadequacy and smoking tobacco reduces penile blood flow by 35 per cent – both of which will reduce your chances of a night of love.

POULTICES FOR YOUR RESPECTIVE LOINS.

You've got to know him quite well for this bit or be a bit forward. But hey, in for a penny in for a pound. Men used to place stinging nettles in their cod-pieces – that would certainly focus his attention!!!! Ginger rubbed on a throbbing shaft also increases its size and just plain rubbing of a throbbing shaft is usually quite effective too. Jasmine will make you feel all tropical and exotic (especially if he rubs it in).

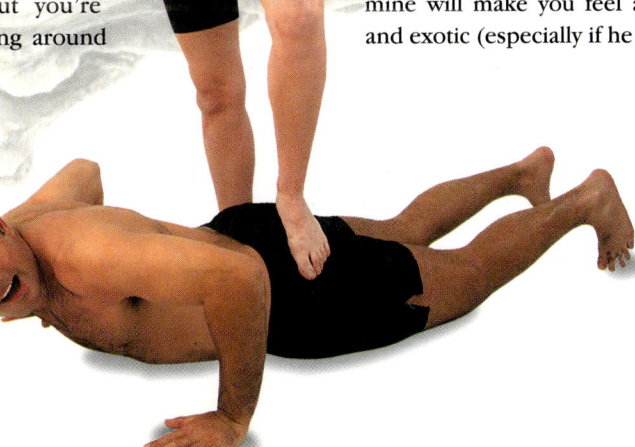

girl*power*

DRESSING to IMPRESS

The sad and simple truth is that men are stunningly Neanderthal creatures sexually. Give them the right visual signals and kpow! Their one-track minds will focus straight on to sex – no conscious thought – well, no thought at all – it's an instant gut reaction: OoOoOo, AHAHAHAH: Me Tarzan, want You Jane.

Which makes the poor dears ridiculously easy to manipulate. Once you've learnt the simple rules of dressing, you can have any man you want. Real women aren't manipulated by the fashion industry – they use fashion to manipulate the men they want straight into bed, straight into the jewellers and florists, and straight into the lawyers to change their wills. To hone your trapping skills, follow these simple rules and use this cut-out-and-keep doll that shows the way men really think. Happy Hunting.

GENERAL RULES

Eccentric touches: men are often scared of sleeping with clever women so they prefer mad or dumb girls, it's scary but true. So put him at ease by wearing a bit of daffy ribbon, a single bizarre earring or a traffic cone on your head.

Reveal & conceal: men like glimpses of what they finally want to possess – a tempting light starter before the main course. So have your skirt just that bit too short to quite reach your stocking top. Almost fall out of your top, but don't, and bend over with straight legs to show a tiny fleck of white pants. It's important to remember to do all these things as if you are totally unaware of doing them and are ever-so-girlishly embarrassed to have inadvertently shown too much.

Easy access: however little or much you're wearing – plan access routes for eager hands. Men like planning driving routes but hate closed off roads or missing motorway turn-offs: YES to poppers, loose buttons, gently-tied bows and keeping your knicker elastic stretchy. Using safety pins to mend a skirt is a definite no-no.

And remember Bucks Fizz.

Dress organically: never try to dress against your body type. Men like women who are confident with their body (they think you'll handle theirs confidently) and there are men who are attracted to every specific type of physicality, just look at the range in pornography: skinny/fat, beautiful/readers' wives, pregnant, hermaphrodite, dwarf, amputee…just make the most of what you've got (or for amputees – what you haven't got).

Shape: tight clothes outline what you've got to offer.

Texture: vary what his hand will run across for excitement: fur, lycra, lace, jelly.

Colour: sends messages:
blue = etheral, orange = warm, red = I'm having my period, tan = American.

Print design: horizontal stripes to widen, vertical stripes to slim and tartan for mystery.

girl*power*

THE DOLL AND WHAT MEN THINK YOU MEAN

CLOTHES
- **Almost see-through vest top**
"Can you or can't you see my nipples?"
- **Micro skirt**
"If I bent over you could just take me here."
- **Jodhpurs**
"I've got a great bum and I'm posh and need taking down a peg or two."
- **Long floaty dress**
"I'm a virgin and you're a big strong deflowerer."
- **Men's suit**
"I'm lesbian but you could cure me."
- **Flowery house-coat**
"I'm just like your mum and I'll look after you."
- **Fur coat, no knickers**
"I'm from the North."
- **Gym slip**
"I need to see the Headmaster."

HAIR
- **Hair in a bun and horn-rimmed glasses (for pulling off)**
"Take off my glasses to see the real me."
- **Pigtails**
"I'm very silly and girly and you could take advantage of me."
- **Long blonde loose hair**
"Drag me to your cave."

UNDERWEAR
- **Wonderbra**
"These are for you."
- **Stockings, suspenders and garters**
"I'm all your Christmases come at once – and you probably will do too."
- **Optional ladder for tights**
"I'm a bit of a slut."
- **Green school knickers**
"I'm a St Trinian's 6th former and very game."
- **Thong**
"I'm already aroused from the friction of the string."

SHOES
Ballet pumps
"I'm small and fragile and need looking after."
Stilettos
"I'm a tottering vision of breasts and buttocks – one touch and I'll cascade."
Strappy shoes
"These little piggies are all chained up for you."

girl*power*

MAKING THE MOST OF SEX MANUALS AND VIDEOS

"Praise be to God who has placed man's greatest pleasure in the natural parts of woman and has destined the natural parts of man to afford the greatest enjoyment of women."

THE PERFUMED GARDEN CIRCA 16TH CENTURY

or (as the British would put it)

"Oooh er Mrs! Don't! – Cooooooooooor! What a great nanosecond, how was it for you darlin'?"

The first quote comes from the famous Arabic sex treatise *The Perfumed Garden* written by Sheikh Nefzawi. It is still one of the most popular sex manuals available today, along with the *Kama Sutra* from India. All these texts are very old, very foreign and very erotic. What a surprise. While other cultures have for centuries considered sexual pleasure to be as vital as eating and sleeping and an art form to be taught and refined, British sexuality is a combination of Christian guilt and Benny Hill.

Thus we have virtually no early manuals and the first Victorian ones are full of warnings and limits. In 1911 Professor G. Stanley Hall wrote that masturbation caused "insanity, blindness, purple clammy skin, dwarfism, dry cough, baldness, stoop, anorexia and digestive problems". More recent books generally read like car maintenance manuals.

It is important to remember the British way to approach all such things – read books in sneaky glances, or standing in shops giggling with your mates and watch videos with the remote control in one hand and your genitals in the other.

BRITISH PEOPLE SUITABLE FOR WRITING BOOKS OR INTRODUCING VIDEOS

- Hip, nauseating couples who will look their best in the gutter-press slanging matches when they divorce.
- Oversexed "clever clever" hippie blokes who have been researching for years on government grants – or, more colloquially, on the dole.
- Weedy male professors who look like they've never shagged and would snap if they did.
- Robust Mother Earth women who are scarily over-enthusiastic, hearty and fecund.
- Blonde, herbal, mystic modern-witches.
- Scary, passion-deflating little old Jewish mothers.

WARNING

If you hold a secret desire to appear in one of these books or videos, or, more alarmingly, your partner is trying to talk you into a starring role – the following points are very important.

RESULTS OF BEING A MODEL IN A SEX MANUAL OR VIDEO

1 Your body will become utterly blemish free and curiously hairless.
2 You will develop a constant faraway look of drugged bliss.
3 You will be able to maintain the most painful positions without sweating, grimacing or saying "Ow, get off, get off, I've got cramp."
4 You will have a name like Vince or Saskia.
5 Despite saying in a brief interview that you used to be very shy and confused about sex, you will romp butt-naked for friends and family and for the world and his wife to see.

USING THE CORRECT TERMS FOR EACH OTHER'S BITS

Indian   Lingam
             Yoni
Chinese Jade Stalk/Stem
             Jade Gate/Pavilion
British Cock *(watercock or tap)*, Devil, Pork Sword, Lollipop, Hot Dog, Hose, Piston, Key, Pudenda *(from Latin pudere, to be ashamed)*, Hell *(Christianity at its best)*, Cauliflower *(sounds like a pub)*, Lucky Bag *(so adult)*, Bun *(post football match snack)*, Drain *(so erotic)*, Cylinder *(romance isn't dead)*.

TANTRIC SEX

This involves special breathing and sexual positions to keep you at the point of orgasm without actually coming – which for women is basically just sex, not tantric sex! Anyway, if it is achieved and you do prevent possible orgasm, energy is sent back into the chakras (the psychic centres of the body) and this can then lead to creativity and occult powers. It's a bit like wine-tasting – put it in, swirl it around a bit, spit it out and think, "um, I've learnt so much, but I'm not drunk am I?"

FOREPLAY

Never commence sexual congress until totally aroused and up for it: for a British bloke, not until you've had fourteen pints and a vindaloo; and for a girl, when you are drunk and desperate enough to be glad that another vertebrate is in your bed, however comatose. Take everything slowly. Footballers need to warm up, and you can't cook a chicken till it's plucked and basted. Start with burning candles, mutual kissing, touching, scratching and oral sex. Medieval Indian Sanskrit texts name many kinds of kiss, scratch and oral sex for both partners, so you should be able to come up with at least one of each.

Romantic PHONE CALLS

Phone companies don't make their money from business or family calls. No, they make it from relationship calls. Asking out, slushy-mush, negotiating a relationship, breaking up and all the advice from friends that has to be given throughout these phases. You can chart a relationship by plotting the number of phone calls to a partner.

Slushy calls mark the peak of affectionate love – they are nauseating, pathetic and interminable but they make you feel warm, wanted and wonderful.

A TYPICAL SLUSHY CALL

Hello, it's me.
Hello me – oooooooo000000.
Have you missed me?
OOOOOoooooh yes – it's been aaaaages since we last spoke xxxxxxx.
Five great biiiiig lonely minutes.
I knooooow, let's never leave it soooo long again.
OOOh no – we might forget what we sound like.
Have you forgotten me already?
OOOOh no – I close my eyes and I see your lovely guinea-pig face.
Eeh, eeh, eeh, eeh.
What are you doing?
I'm being an excited guinea-pig.
Well, I'll bring lots of berries and nuts back for my favourite little excited guinea-pig.
And I'll brush all my fur up into little whorls and polish my tiny front teeth.
OoooooooOOOOOOOO.
AaaaaaAAAAAAAAAAAnyway, I'd better go.
Why, don't you love me anymore?
Of course I do, I adooooooooore you.
OoooooooooooooooOOOOOOOo.
XXXXXXXXXXXXXX.
Bye then.
Bye.
Are you still there?
Yes.
Well, hang up.
Nooooooo, you hang up.
All right, byyyyyye.
Byyyyyyyyye.
You're still there, aren't you?
You do love me, don't you?
Oh, so much it hurts.
XXXXXXXXXXXX.
XXXXXXXXXXXXXXX.
Okay, we'll hang up together – after three – one... two...three...
Are you still there?

girl*power*

GOOD SLUSHY CALLS
Style: Cooing
Content: Little furry animals, bunches of flowers and pretty presents, exotic food and wine, romantic holidays in Paris, clothes worn and facial expressions, pets, longing, size of love, nests.

BAD SLUSHY CALLS
Style: Belching
Content: Pregnancy, housework, depression, fear of death, syphilis, world disaster, torture, your infidelity, constipation.

BAD TIMES TO RING YOUR LOVER FOR A SLUSHY PHONE CALL
- When he's in a board-meeting and the phone's on speaker mode
- When he's drinking with his mates at the Rugby Club
- On a busy but dead quiet train
- When he's seeing his ex-girlfriend for the first time since he dumped her for you
- At his mother's funeral

ALTERNATIVE MODERN VERSIONS OF THE SLUSHY PHONE CALL

ANSWERPHONE MESSAGES
(leave a message in snippets of songs)
- Ev'ry time we say goodbye, I die a little
- I died in your arms tonight
- Have I told you lately that I love you?
- You're the wind beneath my wings
- Hopelessly devoted to you
- It's not what you do it's the way that you do it – that's what gets results

E-MAIL
Send it to him at work – especially if he works in the geology department of an oil company so he has an extra-large computer-screen and your message comes up huge for all to see. Then he'll be really embarrassed and won't be able to get it off the screen for ages.

FAX
Send it to him at work so that it comes out in the general fax-room for everyone to look at, photocopy and distribute.

PAGER
The fun is to see how slushy and rude you can be before the operator sending it gasps.

ELECTRONIC SCOREBOARDS AT FOOTBALL MATCHES
Be really soppy and name him. They'll write a new football chant about him and jokes will be written which will be repeated by his friends until the day he dies.

WAYS OF LETTING HIM DOWN GENTLY

We all make mistakes, but unless you want to end up married to one, you've got to learn how to sort the wheat from the chaff at a very early stage, without causing too much distress. (He knows where you live and might decide to take his angst out on your car.)

This is a very different scenario from the ending of a "long-term" relationship, which involves broken hearts and CD collections. Letting him down gently is the thing you do in the first few weeks, even days, when it is obvious that he is much more keen than you will ever be. In an ideal world this would be long before a physical relationship has developed; however, we all know that it can be this very development that suddenly makes you realize what a terrible choice you've made. The earth didn't move and, in fact, you wished it would open up and swallow you, or him, rather than leaving you to face the inevitable breakfast from hell when he tries to snog you with a mouthful of croissant. (He will be out to impress, even boys know that cornflakes won't do on this occasion.) Consequently, you will try to fall fatally on the butter knife in order to teach yourself a lesson.

HOW DID I GET HERE?

This is the phrase from a great Talking Heads' track that will be playing at double speed in your head, as you drink his coffee and attempt unnoticed, to season it with his whisky. Facing up to the fact that you got here by deliberately ignoring the signs and blinding yourself to your gut feelings, will help you not to do the same ever again, and will also help you to pass the time in the detox clinic. (To think, it all started with that one whisky…)

HE'S SO NICE I MUST FANCY HIM

We have all convinced ourselves of this one, once in a while. He makes you laugh, you talk for hours, you introduce him to your friends and they all tell you he's gorgeous. But when he kisses you, the first thing you want to do is touch-up your lipstick rather than touch-up him. This is the point at which you should be honest with him, and yourself, and not take it a stage further.

I'VE ALWAYS GONE FOR LOOKS, THIS TIME I'LL GO FOR PERSONALITY

Have you ever asked yourself why it is that Mr Zany, life and soul of the party is like that? It's because he has a face like the neighbour's dog and, interestingly, breath to match. One day he will meet a woman who has no sense of smell and quite likes the eager Labrador look. In the meantime, let him lead the karaoke on his own.

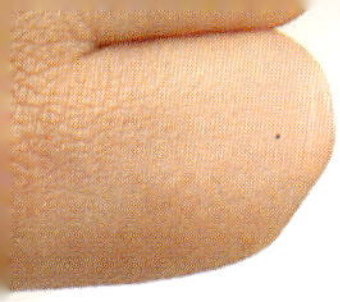

HE REMINDS ME OF MY EX WHO I HAVEN'T GOT OVER YET

Oh dear. This one really is a disaster. Everything he does will remind you of how HE did it much better. An attempt to get over HIM on the rebound can only work if the new man is someone you really fancy and who really is different to the last one.

If you can't do anything but look for a carbon copy, then you should stay at home and breed cats. One day one of them will remind you of one of HIS irritating habits (being sick on your nightdress for instance) and you will be cured.

LETTING HIM DOWN WITH A THUMP
OR HOW NOT TO SAY GOODBYE THE MORNING AFTER...

❝Look, it's all been a terrible mistake, I didn't mean for that to happen, I was drunk, I'm actually celibate. Sorry . . .❞

❝You've been great, I was unsure about my sexuality but you've helped me to realize I definitely am a lesbian.❞

❝That was crap! Get out of my sight!❞

LETTING HIM DOWN GENTLY

The thing to remember is that somehow you have got to try not to hurt his feelings. How was he to know that you wouldn't still fancy him in the morning? After all, he didn't know that you never really fancied him in the first place.

In the normal circumstance of having made a seriously bad bedtime choice (shall it be Teddy or Mr Married but misunderstood? Well Teddy is only a stuffed toy . . .) the way to send him packing without hurting his ego is to wake up, turn to him and say: "I love you, leave your wife, please, please, please . . . I've got a gun." Most men will run for the hills after that kind of breakfast chat.

However, when you have made the dreadful mistake of dropping your standards along with the scanties, then he is going to stick like glue if you offer him the least encouragement (like by still breathing, for instance).

By the way – I'm shagging your BEST FRIEND

HOW TO SAY GOODBYE THE MORNING AFTER

❝God you're so amazing. I didn't know there were men like you. I wish we'd found each other before I met my fiancé. Didn't I tell you about him? He's in the SAS. He's away so much I forget. He should be back later today, maybe you can tell him how we feel about each other, he probably won't kill you...❞

❝That was the best night of my life, I don't know how I'm going to live without you, but my therapist says I'm not ready for a relationship. I'm sorry...will you wait for me? I should be able to make a commitment in about ten years...❞

❝I think I'm in love. I wish I'd never accepted that job in Siberia, perhaps you could come with me, it's only a five-year contract.❞

girl*power*

the rules of JEALOUSY

Unfortunately the more you love someone, the more you will want them to be unaware that any other females populate the planet – except for children, aged crones and disfigured monsters. Your lover may need to have it pointed out to him that all the women he knows, besides you, fall into one of these categories. If you understand these two sentences you have experienced jealousy. Do not worry – this is a much criticized emotion and, at times, very painful but it is as normal to women as sexual insecurity is to men. Recognize jealousy, use its positive effects, accept its negative effects and cure it when it becomes life-threatening to you or to him.

SYMPTOMS

- Green skin.
- Condom counting – VERY sad.
- Words vomiting from your mouth with no thought, as in when he smiles at a girl in a pub – 0.0000000001 of a nanosecond later – "Who's she?" spit, snarl, seethe.
- Phone bill scrutinizing and questions asked in a strange I-have-no-interest-in-this-trivial-detail-but tone, such as "Do we know anyone in Sutton Coldfield, darling?"
- Paranoiac reaction to any change in his behaviour, dress sense or knowledge. "I see you're breathing, I suppose she taught you that."
- Tortuous questioning around what you really want to ask – "So, did you have a nice evening, talk to anyone interesting, get enough sleep, how big was the dent in your mattress, what was the cubic volume of the air needed in your bedroom to support the life-forms there last night...?"

POSITIVE EFFECTS

- Trains you for international espionage by heightening all your senses. It enables you to hear footsteps from several miles distance, see with a telescopic-night-vision-insect-eye-grid facility and smell cheese cooking in Amsterdam.
- Trains you as a "Radio Travel Update Girl". You will know every bus and train timetable, all travel limiting weather conditions and all road works and traffic jams right across the country.
- Gives you a free make-over without having to humiliate yourself on Daytime TV. You will lose weight, cut your hair and improve your dress sense with no effort at all.
- Increases your sex drive and willingness to be experimental. The mere thought of going on a diet makes any girl ravenous.
- It's a perfect test of how much he loves you. If he's unsure of his feelings you will scare him off, but if he loves you he'll be pleased and flattered.

girlpower

NEGATIVE EFFECTS
- No one will ever again be able to refer to you with the adjective "cool".
- Torn leg ligaments from leaping at the phone at its first shudder.
- Severe sleep deprivation. Your nights will be choc-a-bloc with waiting for phone calls, guessing where he is and what he's doing, and running through in your mind the film of discovering his infidelity. The ugly confrontation, his unsolved murder, his burial on a windswept hillside (you beautiful and poignant in a stunning black designer number) and your future life as a mysterious and alluring young widow.
- Social ineptness. At any party or social gathering you will be unable to communicate with anyone at all, if you are unsure of where in the room your lover is. You will nod and smile and murmur, "um, aha, really" totally oblivious of what is being said, and your head will be swivelling through 360 degrees constantly as you try to pinpoint his whereabouts.
- Inability to enjoy television with him. Even watching a cartoon you will suddenly explode, "What, what, why did you laugh? Do you like her? Is that what you really want in a woman? Big brown eyes, long fluffy ears and the ability to run in mid-air and use her ears as a parachute? Well I'm sorry I'm not good enough for you".

CURES
- Stay with him twenty-four hours a day.
- Claim he's a large truanting child and have him electronically.
- Leave out large knives and "Stain-Devil-for-cleaning-cheating-boyfriend's-blood".

OR

Change the power dynamic and make him jealous by:

1 Always referring to men you know (no matter how slightly – plumbers, pest control men) by their first name only, using a warm lilt in your voice saying things like: "Oh, he's lovely, he's more than a friend."

2 Laughingly telling him, as if you're not at all interested, that apparently Mark, the office stud, told Susan that he really likes you and asked whether your relationship was going well and whether it was exclusive.

3 Saving any answerphone messages from men who have called during the day. Playing them innocently when you get back home with your lover. (Have them professionally edited to provoke maximum suspicion.)

4 Learning a new sexual trick from books or friends, doing it with him and when he asks where you learnt that, saying: "Oh, I don't know it just came to me."

5 Grabbing the nearest attractive stranger when you see your partner walking towards you in the street and saying: "Don't look surprised, just kiss me as if you're desperately in love with me and then walk away."

girl*power*

MAKING UP *After*
BREAKING UP

Now be absolutely honest – are you SURE you want to? There is a rule of love called The Forbidden But Familiar Rule which states:

> *"In all the time you know him, a boyfriend will look his most stunningly drop dead gorgeous precisely one week after breaking up with him."*

It doesn't matter who left who, whether he's four foot with pimples or if kissing him used to make your skin crawl. One week after the break-up he will walk towards you in a pub like a god emerging from billowing smoke. He will shimmer – his eyes will melt Formica and you will need to touch him more than you needed that first gasp of air when you left your mummy's tummy.

This sensation does NOT mean that you should make up. It is a dangerous time for a girl, when your brain can turn to mush due to self-doubt and weakness of resolve. It could cause you to career off the exciting motorway of your life, down a dead-end road for several years, with a growing number of whining kids in the back seat.

IMPORTANT THINGS TO REMEMBER

1 Getting a boy back takes quite a bit of time and effort (although girls have an amazing Power Rangers transformation when they are really after a boy – which strangely never occurs for work, cleaning or exercise).

2 You broke up for a good reason – his doubts, your doubts, etc.

3 Relationships after break-ups rarely work. After a great ten-second buzz there are the delights of let-down, bitterness, insecurity and the searing sexual jealousy of interim bonking – and that jolly subject will rear its ugly head in arguments for the next... oooooh, billion years.

Still you can always make up, sort your mind out and then dump him again. You'll have upped your image and that first make-up sex session is always mind-blowing. So what the hell, if you can't help yourself — GO FOR IT.

HOW TO GET HIM BACK IF HE DUMPED YOU

✓ Be super-confident, be very busy socially and get on with your career. Up your image with red nails, short skirts and "shag me" shoes.

✓ Sleep around as if it's an Olympic event, especially with his friends, making sure he hears about it. Leave another man's name on your answerphone along with yours and don't return any of his calls.

✓ Kill him, have his body stuffed and keep it propped up in bed – be sure to stuff the most important organ firmly.

✓ Claim to have a serious illness and tell him that your doctor says that the stress of your break-up is escalating your condition and you need him as only he can nurse you back to health. Once he's back, get better slowly and poison him with minute doses of arsenic until he's too weak to leave.

✓ Claim that you were afraid of the depth of your feelings but are now completely ready for the commitment and feel unleashed emotionally and sexually.

✓ Say that you changed the brand of the pill you were taking and that the new brand made you hate him. (Boys believe that hormones actually change our personalities – whereas we girls all know that they just intensify the truth.)

✗ Turn up at his work, thin and dressed like a tramp, weeping uncontrollably and asking, "But why? Why? Why? What's wrong with me?" over and over and then trying to jump out of his office window.

✗ Stockings, cleavage and promises of kinky sex. You'll get a shag but almost as soon as he's coming, he'll be pulling on his trousers and heading for that door.

✗ Remind him that you know where he lives and he knows how extreme you are, and that even if he emigrated, you'd find him and wouldn't stop stalking him. Say this at 5am, wearing a black balaclava, holding a knife and twitching after breaking into his flat from outside (thirty floors up).

✗ Tell him you're pregnant and that you want to have his baby. You have told your family and his, and would he like to come shopping with you this afternoon for baby clothes, a wedding dress and toilet-roll covers.

✗ Capture him and keep him prisoner in the airing cupboard. BUT you will have to do this for the rest of his life and it is technically illegal. He won't be his usual jolly self, may come to loathe you and, sex-mad though men are, he may go off you.

THE RULES OF BODY LANGUAGE

Bodies and actions are truthful. Thoughts and words lie. Knowing and using this basic knowledge can really pep up a girl's love-life. Bodies react organically to stimuli at a gut level (and below!). Whereas minds react via a duplicitous sieving mechanism of morals, rules, religion, class, fashion, ulterior motives etc ... yawn, yawn.

For a really explosive and fulfilling love-life, forget tortured thoughts and go for gut intuition about yourself and others every time – sexually, emotionally and commitment-wise.

A ridiculous amount of pseudo-scientific guff has been written on this subject since the 1960s, most famously by Desmond Morris – all pointing out the absolutely bloody obvious. Here's a brief synopsis of the really useful stuff you can learn to stop kidding yourself. Come to recognize lying bastards by their body language and use various techniques to maximize your pulling power.

LISTEN TO YOUR OWN BODY LANGUAGE

Your body tells you what is right for you all the time – just listen to it. When it likes the life you are leading it will feel healthy, luscious and super-sensuous, and when it doesn't it will feel tired, listless and stalely sluggish. Your body will react to what job you do, where you live – everything. But the biggest stimulus is who you sleep with and spend time with – so learn to read the signals your body is screaming at you and you'll know who's right for you.

Staying with a bloke you don't really fancy, love or respect, or who treats you badly, will make you subtly ill and exhausted. Don't do it, because the longer you do, the deader and iller you will feel. Ignore your crappy mind when it says, "but everyone else thinks he's great, I should stick by him, he can't cope alone, but love is for ever, but I'll never find anyone else" etc. etc. . . . Fiddlesticks – if your body's collapsing, pack up, get out and get living.

Alternatively, if you meet a bloke who makes you feel excited, sexy, warm and wonderful – but your mind says, "but he's not classically good-looking, my mother wouldn't approve, but I'm in a safe-if-dull relationship now, he's not my class, my religion, dressed right", go with your guts – you'll have great sex, a real relationship and a new spring in your step and sparkle in your eye.

HOW TO SPOT A LYING BASTARD

It's pretty damn easy to tell if a bloke wants sex with you, but he may make lots of promises about commitment, not having a wife or some little thing like six kids. When he's talking check to see if he does any of the actions listed below: they are scientifically known as "non-verbal leakage", or more colloquially "deceit worthy of death". If he does – be careful. If necessary video him with your camcorder and analyze the tape with your girlfriends.

- The shortfall smile where the corners of his mouth go up but there's no warmth there (common in politicians and royalty).
- Avoidance of eye contact – shifty bastard.
- Stiff body posture – sometimes hard to spot and boys can be so gawky naturally.
- Mouth covering – his body is honest even if his mind isn't and it wants to stop the stream of lies.
- Nose touching – very clear sign of lying – he tries to cover his mouth and then deflects his hand to his nose, trying to hide its aim.
- Decrease in frequency of small hand gestures – his body refuses to back up his statements with gestures.
- Increase in body shifts – called squirming.
- Increase in hand shrugs – his body is disclaiming his words, trying to warn you.

- Sweaty palms – that is just plain fear (and quite right) – wait until you work out why he's lying.
- Giveaway momentary facial expressions – can be caught on camera between changes of expression and you will see the true leering letching lying pig. You may not see it consciously in real time but your body will sense it and you will just "know" not to trust him. Go with your gut and walk away.

HOW TO USE THE RULES OF BODY LANGUAGE TO SHOW ATTRACTION
(and recognize it)

Complex body language is used by humans looking for sex because we are trying to find great orgasmic sex for definite pregnancy and a strong long-lasting bond for the nurturing of children. Contraception and careers let us gals sample sex, love and babies separately, but whether you are looking for a mind-blowing bonk or long-lasting love and babes, body language will help you get the best of what you want.

A boy's interest in you is pretty obvious: hard-ons, letching and out-of-the-ordinary kindness, interest in your life, and cleanliness! He will also employ some of the more unisex features in this picture showing signs of attraction – depicted here in a woman so that you can learn to accentuate the signs in order to attract a boy.

N.B. *Be careful not to overdo them or do too many at once – you will look truly gross.*

EYES: TINY GLANCES FOLLOWED BY GAZE BEHAVIOUR TO
a) constantly check each other's reactions
b) hold attention
c) allow mirroring of other's actions and posture

HEAD: NODDING

HAIR: FALLING OVER EYES FOR FALSE MODESTY

CHEEKS: BLUSHING (BIG ROSY CHEEKS)

MOUTH: SMILING (THE JOKER MOUTH)

TONGUE: LOLLING SYMBOLIC PHALLIC TONGUE À LA MICK JAGGER (VERY LONG & POINTY – REPTILIAN)

HANDS: AUTO CONTACT "I WANT TO BE TOUCHED AND PREENING OF HAIR"

STOMACH: DRAWING IN BREATH TO DECREASE WAIST AND ACCENTUATE BOTTOM AND BREASTS

EYEBROWS: RAISED, OVER WIDE EYES (VERY WIDE EYES LIKE SAUCERS)

LEGS AND ARMS: APART WITH NO PROTECTIVE BARRIER SIGNALS

CROTCH: MOMENTARY DISPLAYS FOR GUIDE SIGN

CLOTHES: WEAR LESS TO REDUCE TABOO AREAS AND GIVE OVER-EXPOSURE SIGNS OF AVAILABILITY (VERY SHORT SKIRT)

KNEES: BENDING, WHICH MIMICS ROUND BUTTOCKS

**CHILDISH BEHAVIOUR TO EXCITE PARENTAL PROTECTIVE DRIVES AND PROVIDE REMOTIVATION (GOO GOOING FROM THE BRAIN)

girl*power*

ROLE MODELS *in* LOVE

From the earliest years of reading *Jackie* magazine, we girls have relied on celebrity role models to teach us how to find the perfect partner. This remains true today. We love to see show-business couples as an ideal. Here is a cross-section of the star couples and the women who made it happen.

TOM CRUISE & NICOLE KIDMAN

LIAM GALLAGHER & PATSY KENSIT

Top show-business couple, he's got the teeth and she's got the hair. Nicole, being no fool, had a choice between working in off-Broadway shows and trying to get her break in Hollywood or marrying the biggest star in films. Nicole did the right thing and long may she prosper.

★ ★ ★

No stranger to showbiz marriages, Patsy has already been married to a bloke from Big Audio Dynamite who wasn't the singer and Jim "Alive and Kicking" Kerr from Simple Minds, who were that band that sounded quite like U2 six or seven years ago. She has learned to move with the times and has hitched her wagon to the singer from current Britpop sensation Oasis. Patsy is a dedicated follower of fashion to whom we should pay homage.

girl*power*

DAVID COPPERFIELD & CLAUDIA SCHIFFER

To many observers, getting off with Claudia Schiffer remains the best trick in David's repertoire. Fabulous supermodel Claudia can have her pick of men, so why the smarmy magician? Clue: highest paid entertainer in America. Let's face it, modelling has a limited lifespan and you have to plan for your old age. Well done Claudia.

CLARK KENT AND LOIS LANE

Every young girl's dream is to be the girl who gets Superman. In the films we are so envious of Lois Lane who actually gets off with him. As we get older and get out of our habit of falling in love with unattainable aloof men we realize the double whammy – Lois gets to have the good guy too – Clark Kent. For all that gorgeous hunky Superman is gorgeous and hunky, Clark is sensitive, caring and kind and has the same fantastic physique beneath the suit. Well done Lois, you may be a fictional character but you are still a role model for many generations.

BRUCE WILLIS AND DEMI MOORE

Demi knew all along what none of us had suspected, that Bruce Willis isn't an ageing action film has-been but a talented actor with a well-developed sense of comic irony, as displayed in *Pulp Fiction*. As his career has been rejuvenated thanks to the kindness of Mr Tarantino, it takes the pressure off Demi somewhat. After all, for how much longer are film-makers going to pay her $12 million to get her kit off? Even worse, what will she do if they offer her more to keep them on? She will have to go to hubby for acting lessons. A husky voice and an ability to shed your clothes at will do not an actor make. Demi need not worry, Bruce is fashionable again and so they will live happily ever after.

A Guide to Love Poems

Obviously once you are in a relationship it is easy to lose the romantic element. This is primarily because once he is involved with you he assumes that no more effort is required. You, on the other hand, will expend most of your charm and energy in trying to get him to flush the toilet and remember your name. But you love him and you want to recreate the hearts and flowers of the first couple of months. You remember? The time when he couldn't do enough for you. Lovey dovey phone calls, turning up on time. He used to make you tapes of love songs that reminded him of you. Now he thinks belching along to Wet Wet Wet songs is the height of humour.

The love poems you write, therefore, reflect the various stages of a relationship. Initially, of course, your poems will make no sense at all because you are still at the stage of cuddly nickname and baby language. They will normally go something like:

> *I wub oo squidgy bum*
> *I hope oo wub me too*
> *Your tiggle bear would be so sad*
> *Without her squidgy woo*

Yes, it is a sad state of affairs. The early lobotomized writing of the lovestruck. At the end of your life, the memory of such behaviour will be a source of comfort that death is near. On no account must you let him keep them. Steal them back and burn them once the relationship hits the rocks.

Valentine's Day is a traditional time to write love poetry of the "Roses are red" variety. While it is okay to stick to the time-honoured format, it is worth making the effort to personalize it.

> *Roses are red*
> *Violets are blue*
> *I don't take sugar*
> *But I quite like you*

Very sensible, nothing too icky and you can save your best work for more spontaneous displays of affection. For instance while suffering from PMT. Like most women during this time you will be feeling a bit insecure and ugly, not to say psychotic.

In this case the same format applies only more to the point:

Roses are red
Violets are blue
If you ever leave me
I will kill you

This can be explained away later as a joke when you are in a less fractious state of mind.

There are often situations when you want to drop a little hint to your partner without upsetting him. Poetry can be a useful tool on these occasions. You can make your point without actually throwing things. For example:

I love you very much
You really are so sweet
And I love you even more
When you put down the toilet seat

Simple, but effective. Other variations include:

You are my very own sweetheart
My lovely buttercup
And oh how happy I shall be
When you do the washing up

As things deteriorate in a relationship, poetry is often used to try to infuse some romance back into the relationship. All good love songs are about lost love and it is often tempting to pinch some of the lyrics e.g. "Baby baby where did our love go?", "You've lost that loving feeling" etc. Classic songs for people who cannot express themselves adequately. Try to be more original, as in:

Our love seems to have gone away
You don't seem to have much to say
Try to save it if you can
Or you will die a lonely old man

You see, in that way you are giving him a chance to put everything right while showing him how empty and meaningless his life would be without you.

If all this is to no avail, then there are the poems for leaving a relationship. Back to a familiar theme as you no longer feel like bothering to put in any particular effort:

Roses are red
Violets are blue
I'm seeing your best friend
And no longer want you

Short and to the point and you can therefore avoid a scene. Finally if you are really lazy, you can always pinch a song lyric.

Nothing compares to you
Rather favourably actually

There you are! Even shorter and just about says it all.

LOVE AND ROMANCE IN NOVELS

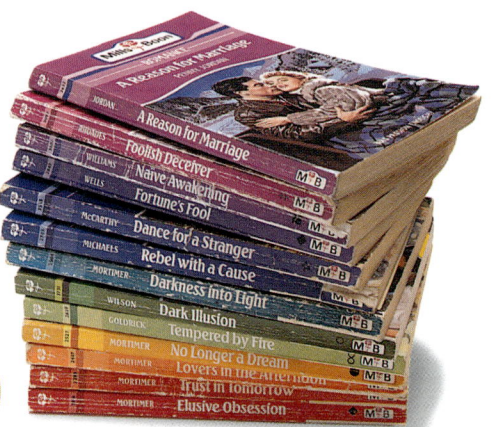

When you first invite a new man into your home, it is important that you set the scene for him. Don't leave him to guess, as he will probably just become fascinated by the bright light and will be confused when presented by other stimuli. If he starts to glaze over and drool, whistling is quite a good way of getting him to focus in the direction that you require.

Assuming that he can read (you can check this by asking him how to spell Pamela Anderson), you can give him clues as to the future nature of your relationship by leaving a romantic novel lying strategically placed by your bed. Depending upon his level of intelligence you may only need to go to the bathroom while he peruses the room, or you may need to build an extension on to your house and then go to Kenya on safari, before you return to ascertain what he has learned.

You may also need to leave one or two even more strategically placed novels where he is more likely to find them, i.e. your knicker drawer, handbag or in between your collection of football programmes from the 1960s (which you have borrowed from your brother especially for this occasion).

TOM JONES

1

We'll start with one of the first classic novels in the English language.

Tom Jones by Henry Fielding is an 18th-century epic novel, as well as a Welsh man who still wears leather trousers under the misguided illusion that he might still get a shag because he used to sound a bit like Elvis, even though he is older than God and a bit tragic. *Tom Jones* the novel is extremely long and a bit dull but the interest for all students of romance is seduction through food. The literary equivalent of the cliché that the way to a man's heart is through his stomach. This involves seduction scenes over huge food feasts – very much for traditionalists and women who do not want to be called a pig because they have a penchant for cake. The idea of food and sex being connected will liberate you forever, and if he is a bit rubbish at least you've had a good meal.

Message to boyfriend: Don't comment on the size of my bum or you will never get a shag again.

WUTHERING HEIGHTS

2

This fabulous story of lost love and tragedy is a romantic ideal for all girls. All women fall for the mean and moody, dangerous type of bloke. That's because he's unpredictable and exciting and you are prepared to put up with the tantrums and unreliability because you will cure his pain and you will both live together happily ever after. Of course, after a while, like Cathy, the heroine of the story, you might get a bit fed up and go for the nice guy who is totally devoted, but as dull as the Lottery Show on a Wednesday with

girl*power*

Carol Smilie. In the end he is so boring, that Cathy would rather be dead and spend eternity haunting Heathcliff, the git who forced her into the arms of Mr Pipe-and-slippers in the first place.

> ***Message to boyfriend:*** Mess me about and you will never sleep again without hearing Kate Bush shrieking outside your window.

MILLS AND BOON NOVELS

Every single Mills and Boon novel is a modern-day version of *Wuthering Heights*. It may be set in Kent or Kenya, but the basic plot is always: a woman with a veiled past, who encounters a moody dark-haired man who is very rude to her and she hates him, whilst fighting a weird attraction. Then she meets his brother who is blond, blue-eyed and a bit thick but very nice to her, so she decides to go out with him. Then she finds out that the dark-haired obnoxious brother has had some kind of personal tragedy which has made him bitter, so she marries him instead.

> ***Message to boyfriend:*** I don't mind if you don't do the washing up as long as there is a trauma in your past to excuse it.

BARBARA CARTLAND NOVELS

Romantic stories of gentrified courtship, hearts and flowers. Women in huge pink dresses and quite large hair being courted by men in the old-fashioned way. No subtlety involved, so any man can understand what you are getting at.

> ***Message to boyfriend:*** No sex until marriage or I'm actually ninety and related to royalty, but don't look it because I bathe in the blood of virgins.

CATHERINE COOKSON NOVELS

Very similar premise to Barbara Cartland books except with a Northern working-class setting. A similar deal of virtuous young women being pursued by gentlemen. In this case, however, the heroine will have lost most of her family to plague and pestilence and will have been beaten by father/landlord/boss so she will be a bit cynical and the man will have to work a bit to gain her affections.

> ***Message to boyfriend:*** I'm no fool even though I'm not posh, so watch yourself.

JACKIE COLLINS NOVELS

Be careful with this one. They deal with very precarious romance. A modern-day equivalent of the above in many respects. A beautiful girl from the wrong side of the tracks is used and abused by men. She then usually makes a fortune by way of her talent or beauty and is very cynical about men while retaining a certain charming vulnerability. On the other hand she is often completely evil and wants to wreak revenge on every man she meets.

> ***Message to boyfriend:*** You are the man who can save me from myself or Oh dear! You've seen me naked. Now you must die!

LOVE AND ROMANTIC HEROES

There have been many romantic heroes throughout history, both fictional and real from Don Juan to Johnny Depp. Johnny Depp as we all know, only goes out with women who look like they have a heroin dependency, so maybe we should forget about men who prefer stick insects and look a bit further afield.

First we should look at fictional romantic heroes as they are the ideal, the writer can give them all the qualities that he or she desires. Similarly it is the tendency of girls to project what we really want on to the men we actually have. But there are pitfalls even in the romance of the imagination.

FICTIONAL ROMANTIC HEROES

MR ROCHESTER

The romantic hero from *Jane Eyre* is a good example as he fell in love with Jane, who let's face it, wasn't much of a looker and then became blind. But of course he deserved a break because his first wife was as mad as a hatter and he had to lock her in an attic. Jane, on the other hand, was quite relieved, as she didn't have to dress up and if she had a bit of PMT he found it quite easy to deal with. So if you are a bit of a lazy baggage, he would be a dream come true. Also it meant that if he got on Jane's nerves, she could poke him with sticks for a laugh.

ROBIN HOOD

On first impressions Robin of Sherwood appears to be quite a catch. He's very handsome and athletic and he obviously has a very highly developed sense of decency, stealing from the rich to give to the poor and all that. However, this of course means he is not really suitable if you happen to be wealthy in the first place, as he will be forever going through your purse to give your credit cards to the homeless and needy.

BATMAN

Similarly, all very good in principle. What with the leather outfit and the fight for truth, justice and the American way. Also Batman has that pained vulnerability of a man who is too shy to approach a woman without wearing a mask. The downside, of course, is that if you meet a man in disguise who won't tell you his name, you can usually safely conclude that he is a stalker or he is married. Either way, if he explains himself by informing you that he is a superhero, you can only assume that he's full of delusions or if he is telling the truth, that there is no future in dating a man who works all hours for no pay. What a loser!

ROMEO

The most romantic hero of them all. Fell in love with the daughter of his family's sworn enemies and was prepared to die rather than be parted from her. We have all envisaged that balcony scene happening to us, where the man of our dreams comes to us at night declaring undying love. Of course he could have phoned which would have been a lot more civilized, particularly in the middle of the night in winter. Also if you were Juliet, you would have to think twice before topping yourself just because your mum had banned you from seeing that lad you'd snogged once, when you were only fourteen.

FACTUAL ROMANTIC HEROES

These can be taken these days from any area of the media – showbusiness, sport or royalty.

HUGH GRANT

Hugh is seen as the archetypal English gentleman. Despite his great versatility as an actor, he does tend to end up playing the dippy, inbred, aristo type. The great thing about going out with Hugh Grant would be that if you went to a première with him, wearing an interesting dress, then you would immediately become more famous than him. The downside of course is that you would worry a bit when he said he was "just popping out for a spin in the car"… at about midnight.

PAUL GASCOIGNE

The Clown Prince of football. What a cheeky chappy, always japing and exhibiting that boyishness that makes us girls want to look after him. You'd always have a laugh and a big house, but the downside is when he would accidentally, just for a laugh, break your face with a punch.

PRINCE CHARLES

What could be more romantic than marrying a prince? Apart from marrying Noel Edmonds of course. We all watched the fairy-tale wedding of Charles and Diana and wished it was us, only regretting his large ears and general ugliness. But, taking that into account and his age and dullness, he would still seem like the catch of the century. The future King of England has chosen me! How much more excited could you be? You would feel on top of the world. That is, of course, until you realize that the woman he really wants looks like an old man with a face like a bag of spanners.

JARVIS COCKER

A true hero among men. Leader of fantastic pop group Pulp. Not only magnificently talented but also a bit of a hard man. Forget the nerdy look, he took on Michael Jackson at the Brit Awards by disrupting his performance and was charged with assaulting children. Tragic irony.

N.B. The thing to remember about romantic heroes is that they too fart and burp and we should not forsake the ordinary nice boys who would treat us beautifully in favour of a fantasy that does not exist in reality.

THE DO'S AND DON'TS OF Office Romance

There is a song that says, "The first cut is the deepest." There is a similar, lesser-known but equally poignant phrase, "The first job is the grimmest." Now for many a girl about town, the first job after school or college is as an office junior: and really, no matter what your skills and qualifications, it will be junior (unless daddy owns the company).

When you are asked to draw a diagram of your position in the company you will be at the bottom under the title "asexual polyp" (the lowest known form of life). So to assuage the inescapable boredom and frustration, you will inevitably cast your eye around for prospective mates. You will, however, not be alone since everybody else in the office, whether they have been working there for ten minutes or ten years will be doing likewise, because the boredom and frustration of the office only gets worse the longer you are there and the higher up you go.

When you first arrive, every man in the office will strike you as a sad, dull loser. However, there is an insidious disease that sets in fairly quickly, which in scientific terms is known as "Confined Space Syndrome". CSS is best described as a situation where you are stuck on a lifeboat with a small group of people and you have almost given up hope of survival. You become very attached to your fellow travellers and suddenly they are the focus of your world. Therefore anything that they say or do becomes fascinating and attractive. Similarly, if you are spending eight hours a day filing, typing, sorting post or answering the phone, your brain atrophies to the extent that any source of distraction becomes a major pleasure.

The potential risk guys are as follows:

YOU HAVE BEEN WARNED!

THE LEAST UGLY MAN IN THE OFFICE
If you met this guy at a party you would puke in your purse. However, in the context of CSS, that is, in a room full of pond scum, a toad can assume the attractiveness of Brad Pitt. The "Least Ugly Man" therefore is a bit of a catch and unfortunately he knows it, although sadly he doesn't know why. This means that you will jump through hoops to get him to notice you, and eventually he will take time out from photocopying his arse to ask you for a date and you will both think he is doing you a favour. It is only when you get him out of the office environment that you realize what a hideous goon he is and you will run away screaming. Unfortunately this will have happened to him on every other previous date and he will metaphorically cling on to your leg until you leave the job.

THE FUNNY WEIRD GUY
On your first day at the office some kindly soul will warn you to steer clear of "Funny Weird Guy". He will latch on to you straight away as you are new

blood. He has a macabre sense of humour and hates everybody in the office and the world. Now after a stultifying first week in your job you begin to identify with him and his warped cynicism assumes a Woody Allenesque appeal. But you were warned. Gradually you will discover that he is forty-five and still lives with his mother (who died in 1978) and when you have become established as the only other living being that he can communicate with, he will become obsessive. Once he starts bringing you gifts of dead woodland animals, there is nowhere for you to go other than back to the recruitment office. (You may also need to move house.)

THE OTHER NEW GUY

This may at first seem quite promising. You have something in common. You are both new and a bit nervous and are both outsiders. So naturally you will start going to lunch together or walking to the bus stop so that you can compare notes on progress and offer each other moral support. This might insidiously lull you into a false sense of security. It is only when you start to explore more personal areas of conversation that you learn he is still an air cadet at the age of twenty-three and owns every record that Phil Collins has ever made.

THE PATERNAL CARING GUY

This could be your boss or a co-worker who has been with the company for a while. He will be a good bit older than you and initially seem like an oasis of sense and maturity in a sea of chaos. He will be very patient with you while you learn the ropes and seem miraculously available at all times to give you advice and guidance. After a while he will suggest a drink after work so that he can explain more about the job and the company to you, if you like. And there you have it: The Married Serial Shagger.

THE ENIGMATIC SHY MAN

Now here is a challenge. In the depths of boredom you will inevitably find yourself drawn to this man. He has been with the company for twelve years, yet none of his co-workers know anything about him. Every approach you make to get to know him will be rejected, which will of course, make him appear even more intriguing. But you will never solve the mystery because he is a serial killer from Luton!

AND FINALLY... OFFICE PARTIES

Despite all advice to the contrary you will inevitably end up at the office Christmas party, and having drunk your own body weight in tepid Liebfraumilch, will shag any or all of the above.

girlpower

THE RULES OF DIVORCE

As Tammy Wynette once said, so succinctly: "Our D.I.V.O.R.C.E. is final today." She spelt out the word "divorce" because she was afraid that the C.H.I.L.D.R.E.N. might realize what was going on. Now, given Tammy's age, it would be safe to assume that the said offspring would be at least twenty years old, that they were a bit special or that she was as cracked as an egg. However, if her children were infants, the fact that daddy was suddenly not living with them may have given them a clue. That said, the message is very clear – divorce is a messy business. Do not take it lightly and don't do it unless you are absolutely sure, and are married, otherwise you could be causing a lot of heartache for no good reason.

There are many reasons for wanting a divorce

1 You no longer wish to be married.
2 He forgot your birthday and therefore has to be punished.
3 You were drunk when you got married and you have now sobered up and realize that you made a terrible mistake.
4 You have met someone you like better.
5 You can't quite put your finger on it, but he is generally a bit rubbish.
6 You got married for a bet but a joke's a joke, you need to move on now.

Divorce is similar to dumping someone, but a lot more complicated. However, you can draw on past experience in order to achieve it. Don't take that too far though. For instance, when you were ten and you got rid of the boy you played kiss-chase with by telling him he smelled. That was adequate then, but these days it takes a bit more. Although bad body hygiene can be used as a compounding felony, apparently, legally it is not enough in itself to dissolve a marriage, although obviously it should be.

INFIDELITY

This is an easy one, unless it's yours. If he has been unfaithful, you can get rid of him and get to keep everything. If you have cheated, deny it. He can't prove anything without pictures. If you have been stupid enough to show him pictures, then you deserve anything you have to deal with after that. Stupid!

MENTAL CRUELTY

This is quite a goody. This can include anything from him undermining your confidence to watching Anthea Turner on some cutesy pets programme. Other forms of mental cruelty that are acknowledged as grounds for divorce include: listening to records by Phil Collins, Chris de Burgh or Dire Straits more than twice in your lifetime. Also, renting videos that feature Bruce Willis, Pamela Anderson, Sylvester Stallone and particularly Tom Hanks, with special mention for *Forrest Gump*.

Leaving the toilet seat up and the cap off the toothpaste are viewed as major misdemeanours in a modern marriage.

IRRECONCILABLE DIFFERENCES

This is a good one as its terms of reference are quite vague. Make him fill out this questionnaire. If the majority of his answers are "Yes" then you will be single again within weeks:

1. Do women have equal status in today's society?
2. Are women responsible for the upkeep of the home?
3. Is farting in bed and lighting farts appropriate behaviour?
4. Is Sandra Bullock pretty?
5. Do you feel entitled to comment on your spouse's weight/hair/underwear?
6. When your wife is suffering from low self-esteem do you try to jolly her along by telling her to "Pull yourself together, you silly cow?"
7. Do you think that men are innately superior because they can pee up walls?
8. Is it not your considered opinion that Pamela Anderson's breasts are real and if they are not then your wife should get some?
9. Have you often bought your wife kitchen appliances for her birthday/Christmas? And did you think it unreasonable for her to throw them at your head?
10. If you had a son would you insist that he be called Clint, Arnie, Sly or something equally macho so that nobody would think he was a "poof?"

The best way to bring about divorce and keep everything, is to convince him that he should leave you. So, change the locks on the door, burn all his possessions and when he tries to contact you by phone, pretend that you don't speak English.

The biggest insult to a man is to threaten his territorial rights. So, if all else fails, go to a health farm. When you get back, say that you were abducted by aliens and have been impregnated by a huge slug-like creature called Gil.

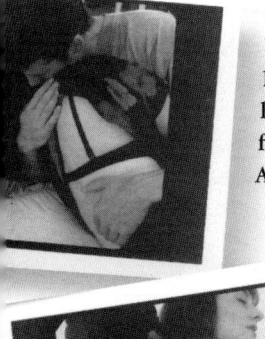

girl*power*

DEALING WITH PROPOSALS OF MARRIAGE

If you have played the mating game particularly well; that is, been supportive, laughed at all his jokes, (you know, generally reminded him of his mother) you may inadvertently attract a proposal of marriage. Now depending upon your point of view, this could be the crock of gold at the end of the rainbow or the realization of all your darkest nightmares.

HOW TO GET ONE:

✓ **Do** play a bit hard to get, i.e. pretend that you have a complete aversion to marriage and intend spending your later years living in an attic with cats, smelling of pee and reading runes. He will see it as a challenge.

✗ **Do not** invite him to your house on the second date and ask him to bring a blood sample and birth certificate. This is playing it just a little too keen.

✓ **Do** try to make yourself completely indispensable to him, possibly by hiding everything he owns.

✗ **Do not** abduct him at gunpoint and tie him to an altar until the priest arrives.

✓ **Do** explain the financial advantages of married couples' tax allowances.

✗ **Do not:** threaten to set fire to yourself unless he names the day.

✓ **Do** let him think it's his idea, after wading through 800 issues of *Hello!*, he may just get on with it.

✗ **Do not** get pregnant. Although a tried and tested man-trap, it's better to buy a dog, he will fall in love with that and never leave you.

girl*power*

51

Advice on how to avoid a proposal of marriage may sound like a joke as we are taught that all men avoid marriage; however, this is not the case at all and for some reason the marrying type always seems to turn up when you least want him. So you need to know the golden rules in the art of avoidance.

HOW TO AVOID ONE

Do tell him that there is congenital insanity in your family.

Do not let him stay overnight in your flat. The cleanliness and nice food will turn his head and you will never get rid of him.

Do pick your nose when you meet his parents. If it's an outdoor occasion, also remember to spit in the street.

Do not invite him to your cousin's wedding, unless she is likely to leave her groom standing at the altar.

Do let him find an ice-pick hidden under your bed.

Do not let him find a cuddly bunny toy in your bed.

Do make him buy your sanitary goods as a foretaste of things to come.

Do not let him get you pregnant.

A GUIDE TO THE TOP SLUSHY FILMS

It's Saturday night, you're in love, you don't need other people. They'll only ruin your fun by having such a good time being single and reminding you of what you're missing. Just say no to parties and wine bars, stay in instead and rent a romantic sloppy video. Cuddle up on the sofa and get down on the shag pile. Dim the lights and chill the ice bucket then fasten your seat belts as you're in for a bumpy ride. Here's our guide to a slushy night in…

THE WAY WE WERE

A realistic romance in which the couple involved are madly in love but can't stand the sight of each other. They have nothing in common and are poles apart politically but does that stop them marrying? No siree. Loads of close-ups of a fabulously sexy and youthful Robert Redford looking stunning in his white naval uniform while poor old Babs has multiple personality hair ranging from World War Two tidal-wave curls to a frizzy Sixties Afro. You don't believe a word of it but the theme tune is sloppy and bound to bring tears to the eyes.
Weepy rating: ¼ box of tissues

WHEN HARRY MET SALLY

Famous for Meg Ryan's faked orgasm scene in a diner. It is rumoured that she had a radio piece in her ear and her agent kept telling her how much money she was earning for the film, until eventually… well, you saw the result. Ah, money – the one true aphrodisiac.
Weepy rating: 1 tissue

SLEEPLESS IN SEATTLE

Weepy widower jettisons to fame after his precocious son phones in to a live radio programme and advertises for a new mom. Most kids his age are looking to swap computer games or dodgy bootleg tapes, but not this boy. He knew what he was missing… clean clothes, cooked meals and a dad who went to work in a decently ironed shirt. Once again Meg "randy" Ryan is only too willing to oblige. Stunning shots of the Manhattan skyline and the fabulously phallic Empire State Building. A happy-ever-after ending and absolutely no sex…
Weepy rating: ¼ box of tissues

BRIEF ENCOUNTER

Desperately coy and English. A respectable couple who are both happily married meet in a station café. When she tells him she has something in her eye he expertly plucks the offending particle from her cornea and they fall madly in love. But this was romance in the clean and wholesome 1940s and when they finally try to get their kit off, they realize they have far too much respect for each other and

instead of bonking, they part for ever, even confessing their forbidden love to their spouses who are very understanding indeed. Well why shouldn't they be, nothing happened.
Weepy rating: ¾ box of tissues

NOW VOYAGER
Frumpy eyebrow-clotted Bette Davis is transformed into a svelte beauty just to spite her hateful mother. She then goes on a cruise and falls in love with a stranger after he lights two cigarettes at once and offers her one. In those days everyone knew how dangerous it was for single women to light their own fags, so his gallantry was greatly appreciated. Once back on dry land, Bette discovers her mystery lover is married with kids, so she bids him farewell and goes home to endure her mother's bitchy comments of "I told you you'd never get a man" until finally telling her to bugger off. Mummy is so furious she stages a heart attack and drops down dead. The film ends with the two clandestine lovers looking out at the night sky and Bette uttering those immortal words "Oh Jerry, don't let's ask for the moon, we have the stars." No one understood it but wept buckets anyway.
Weepy rating: 2 boxes of tissues

THE WOMEN OF WINDSOR
An American movie made for television allegedly about the lives and loves of Di and Fergie, which should be subtitled "Just Say No". It is the perfect antidote to any sickly Cinderella notions anyone may still be harbouring. No the Princesses do not get married and live happily ever after. They wear dreadful clothes, pile on cellulite, develop eating disorders and never really feel safe in a bikini again.
Weepy rating: 1 box of tissues (you'll laugh so hard you'll cry)

LOVE STORY
The ultimate romantic slush puppy film. They're young, they're beautiful, they're in love, they die. (Well, she does but he's moping around so much that he may as well too.) Don't watch this on a first date, you'll reveal your vulnerability all too soon and no doubt ruin the popcorn by sobbing into it.
Weepy rating: a trolley load of tissues from Superdrug

CASABLANCA
A world where snappily dressed men utter immortal lines such as: "Of all the bars in all the towns in all the world, she had to walk into mine." Yet another love story where the lovers can't have each other because it would hurt someone else's feelings and besides there's a war on and isn't that more important than their own selfish yearnings. Here's looking at you kid.
Weepy rating: 1 box of tissues

AN AFFAIR TO REMEMBER
Wear absolutely no eye make-up to see this film or you will emerge looking like a drunken tramp returning home the morning after the night before. Sad, sad, sad. Once again true love conquers all but not before the heroine is maimed in a car crash while on her way to tell her lover she'll marry him. She spends the rest of the film in a wheelchair, keeping her disability a secret from her man and thereby saving him the job of pushing her around all their married life. When he never sees her again he thinks she didn't really love him – wise conclusion, only a true pessimist would think "hang on she's late, perhaps she's been in a car accident". No that didn't cross his self-obsessed mind. Eventually they meet and it all comes out, wheelchair included. They profess undying love then die.
Weepy rating: 3 boxes of tissues and an intensive course of colonic irrigation

*girl*power

HOW TO HAVE A BIT ON THE SIDE AND GET AWAY WITH IT

You're young, you're romantic and you're in love. You spend all your time together and neither of you even look at another member of the opposite sex. All the stars in the heavens are shining brightly, but a word of caution, it might not last. Don't panic, it can happen to the best of us, just beware of the signs of the seven-year itch. Sometimes you don't even have to wait that long, it can be the seven-month itch, the seven-day itch or just plain crabs. In which case one of you has probably already resorted to a bit on the side.

FLIRTING

If you really are bored but don't want to go down the "slapper route", why not try some innocent flirting instead. It's much healthier than binge eating or shoplifting and it does give you the opportunity to dress up. Let's face it, if you are stuck in a long-term relationship, you no doubt live in old sweatshirts and odd socks. What's the point? He doesn't notice you any more. But he soon will if you start flaunting those black lacy mini dresses with nothing but a Wonderbra underneath, especially if you say you're just going to the corner shop. He might even assume you're getting it elsewhere and start making an effort to be a better lover (stranger things have happened).

Sexual fantasies are a useful tool and it's so much nicer to have someone else to fantasize about when making love with your long-term partner. But don't get too carried away and call out their name instead of your boyfriend's or you may just arouse suspicion instead of passion.

GUILT

The most important thing about cheating on your lover is not to feel guilty. You'll end up feeling so miserable with remorse you might be in danger of confessing. This is commonly known as the "getting it off your chest" syndrome. Forget it, it's too late. You should have got it off your chest the moment that hunky sex god climbed on.

But you didn't, so learn to live with it, or the chances are you will have nowhere to live. Telling the truth will not benefit your steady relationship, it will end it. Or worse still, your boyfriend will feel compelled to get revenge by doing the same thing to you, hopefully though with a different person.

DRIVING THE GUILT AWAY

An excellent way of having an affair and getting away with it is to become a driving instructor and only teach men. For a start they won't concentrate on the driving because you are a woman and they simply won't believe that you know how to drive. So you will have their full attention in order to seduce them and still get paid for it. You'll have a portable venue so you can park anywhere (legal) and get lusty on the job. Your boyfriend will assume you're working late and no questions will be asked. Don't leave tell-tale signs in the glove compartment, such as stockings, whips or condoms – he may just put two and two together.

LOVE BEGINS AT HOME

If you're housebound then make the best of it. There's always the washing machine to mend, the windows to clean, the lawn to mow and the bedroom could probably do with a spot of painting and decorating. Shop around until you find the best looking handy men available and quickly employ them. Keep their tea cups topped up and always have something hot and spicy on the cooker, then take advantage of them in every way. Window cleaners make excellent choices as they are aware of all exit routes and have a ladder in case your husband arrives home early without warning.

Firemen are very sexy and also come with their own ladder (not to mention their own hose). But don't do anything too dramatic to get their attention. Setting fire to the chip pan can go wrong and instead of a fiery afternoon of passion you might just find yourself responsible for the death of the family next door and wind up with an arson and manslaughter charge slapped on you. It's safer to feign the old cat-caught-up-a-tree scenario; simply answer the front door in your underwear and cry a lot.

Way back in the 1960s frustrated couples discovered the joys of the gallantly named wife-swapping parties. They daren't call them husband-swapping parties because women aren't stupid; let's face it, if they're going to swap their husband they'll get something decent like a new dishwasher not another bloody husband. The parties were a hit though; picture if you can, a group of respectable men and women all dressed in kaftans, drinking gallons of punch, nibbling canapés then getting off with each other. At least this way you had your partner's permission to be unfaithful and nobody got hurt. Unless of course, no one wanted to swap with you. Then you would have to sell up and move to where the locals are even uglier.

Finally there's always the old harmless cybersex routine. Make a connection on the Internet and tip-tap your way to ecstasy. As you lie about your looks you can relax in the certain knowledge that he is doing the same thing. Don't think about what he really looks like, just imagine your own Adonis and go for it. If your typing skills are above average you may even achieve orgasm simultaneously.

WARNING
- Never cheat on your lover with anyone he may know – one of the blokes from the pub or a neighbour is a recipe for disaster. You will be discovered sooner or later.
- Never confide in a close personal friend then borrow her best jacket and leave it on the bus. She will be so furious her only alternative will be to ruin your life by spilling the beans on your sordid little liaison. (See any soap opera plot on television.)

THE TELL-TALE SIGNS
IF YOU DON'T WANT TO BE CAUGHT OUT THEN REMEMBER THESE SIGNS
- Destroy all incriminating e-mail messages
- Don't buy a see-through black lace shirt then wear it to clean the car
- Don't apply full make-up when you've told him you're just going for a swim
- Don't let him see any new lingerie you buy
- Hide all crotchless knickers
- Don't make any calls from home that can be traced on your bill, and have the 1471 trace-code removed from your line
- If he suddenly tells you how sexy you are, beware, he is onto something
- Don't let him see you naked, you may have the odd scratch
- Look behind you any time you leave the house in case he has a private detective trailing you
- Don't wear too much perfume

Good luck!

THE TRUTH ABOUT FAIRY-TALE LOVE

Ha, baa, humbug – as if, come on, it doesn't exist. Love does, desire and companionship do, even happy faithful marriages do – but not all that fairy-tale tosh us girls grew up with. We were raised to want to be princesses and the dictionary definition of a princess is the wife of a prince! – Get away! Nowadays we can achieve, on our own, all the things that previously we could only have got through husbands: power, position, money, safety, children and sex on tap – as Gloria Steinem the US feminist said: "Some of us are becoming the men we wanted to marry."

So, what we want from men now is proper equal love. BUT, not so fast, not so cocky – we must consider fairy-tale love because, let's be honest, in her heart of hearts even the most sane, most capable, well-off, career-minded, multi-friended, sussed hip chick still occasionally succumbs to the dream of the knight in shining armour who solves everything, for ever and ever, amen...

CURRICULUM VITAE – Ye Olde Prince

Height: Taller than you but not gangly
Looks: Dark, handsome and brooding
Voice: Deep and moistening
Tongue: Large, with Duracell batteries
Skin: Soft, luscious, hairy and clean
Clothes Sense: Shining armour, classic style with individual touches
Favourite Phrase: "You taste wonderful"
Vehicle: Steed
Date of Birth: Two years older than you
Marital Status: Single, a virgin, but great in bed
Income: Untold riches and mounting
Intellect & Education: Clever, complex and worldly wise, well-read in arts, sciences, Mrs Beaton and cleaning fluid labels, can change plugs and nappies, and understand tax loopholes and your mind
Qualifications: Birthright and folklore
Career to Date: Being lonely, ruling his kingdom as wisely as Solomon, saving children, scoring goals, winning cases, releasing hits, starring in films and dreaming of meeting you and keeping you ecstatic
Hobbies: Waking heavy sleepers with a kiss, shoe fetishism, climbing up girls' hair, making sour-faced girls laugh, solving riddles on pain of death, running singles' nights for foreign princesses
Aspirations: Continued wise kingdom-ruling with excerpts of his life used in Hero aftershave adverts, living happily ever after with you.

HOW TO RECOGNIZE FAIRY-TALE LOVE

- Instant absolute KPOW! attraction – eyes out BOING! on stalks
- Visible Ready Brek glow and the sensation of weightlessness
- *Carmina Burana* when you see him, Puccini when you kiss
- Can't nibble or snooze or think of anything but HIM, wedding dresses and curtains
- Nausea, swooning, shortness of breath and heart flutters
- Even burping and nail-biting is attractive if he does it
- Your womb will positively bubble with hormones and lubricants

ALTERNATIVE EXPLANATION FOR THESE SYMPTOMS

You've got flu while having your period and he works in the chemist.

POSSIBLE OBJECTS FOR FAIRY-TALE LOVE

For Him
- Women – if ideal it'll be fleeting
- His mother – his blue-print for the ideal woman
- Cars – constant expenditure of money and time apparently okay
- Arsenal – constant forgiveness apparently okay
- Beer – infinitely desirable despite many late night rejections
- Catalogued *Razzle* collection – sex and ordering – male heaven

For Her
- Men – if ideal it'll be soul destroying
- Best friend – loves you for you despite numerous long rejections for worthless blokes
- Pets – can't talk back and can always be destroyed
- Cake – always fulfilling and can't run away
- Shoes – arched, spiked and mute
- Romantic fiction – let's avoid reality – this is female heaven

N.B. *Always remember Fairy-tales can become Cautionary Tales and Horror Stories:*
Fairy-tales always end with the first kiss or the wedding. Ideally they should have a ten-year update, when the prince has gained two stone, spends most of his nights out with the knights and has a second damsel set up in her own castle down the road. Meanwhile the princess is sick of washing royal socks, fancies ruling a kingdom of her own and finds glass slippers less than ideal for swollen pregnant ankles.

FINDING LOVE AT THE DATING AGENCY

So you've tried the pub, the gym, even your brother's mates and yet you're still single, looking for love and every bloke you meet is a loser or married or both. You look at your old maiden aunt all alone with sixteen cats and a flat that stinks of wee and you think "that'll be me one day". Well, don't despair, there is still hope, making contact with a potential lover through a dating agency or lonely hearts ad does not necessarily mean you're sad, ugly and desperate. On the contrary it shows you are a girl who knows what she wants and where to find it – so go for it! But do remember, when people ask where you met your lover, whatever you do, don't tell them the truth, they will only assume you are sad, ugly and desperate.

Dating agencies promise to team you up with your ideal partner. A "you say tomato, I say tomato" sort of perfect match. Compatibility is their motto. You hand over all your personal information before meeting your date which cuts down on time-wasters and one-night-stand seekers. Or so they say.

HANDY HINTS

Draw up a list of all your good points, lie if you have to, you are doing this for yourself after all. Then compile a list of requirements that your dream man should have. Do not write "must be Keanu Reeves", you will only be disappointed.

Have your photograph taken by one of those glamour photographers who promise to make everyone look like a Hollywood film star (and let's hope they don't include Babe in their portfolio). Send in your fabulous *Hello!*-style photo and wait for the deluge of mail. Remember, you will know it's you even if it doesn't look anything like you and what's more you could prove it in a court of law if that became necessary.

Just ask your mother to bear witness, no doubt she has always wanted to see you looking nice, so naturally she'll be on your side.

THE DATING AGENCY LIE DETECTOR

HE SAYS	HE MEANS
• Committed Christian teetotaller	Psychotic serial killer
• Bearded and balding	Unbelievably dull with a personal hygiene problem
• Enjoys country walks	As poor as a church mouse
• Professional home owner	You're not getting a penny
• Seeks beautiful blonde-haired, leggy goddess	I'm pig ugly
• Looks aren't important	I'm desperate
• Perseus, seeks fair maiden for steamy nights on Mount Olympus	Nutter

girl*power*

Safety precautions to bear in mind when looking for love at the dating agency

1 Meet in a public place and we don't mean a lavatory.

2 Go with a trusted friend who won't take the piss, then have her wait outside the chosen rendezvous with a pair of binoculars and a mobile phone.

After ten minutes have her call you with her opinion of the date. If she likes the look of him then stick around but ask her to arrive unexpectedly and join you. If she doesn't approve then hang up tearfully and tell him there's been a death in the family and you have to leave immediately. When he asks if he can see you again, say that even though you do like him enormously, you couldn't possibly meet him again as the memory of this sad and painful occasion would only cloud any potential future relationship you may have. If he believes that, you know you must have made the right decision.

3 If the dating agency asks you to sign a dodgy-looking contract and part with thousands of pounds, don't do it. Ask them first if you can see proof of their success rate (wedding photos or letters of gratitude from happy couples).

Scrutinize these items closely: photos can be faked. Take great notice of the handwriting, does it look like it may have been written by someone with a mental problem or undergoing a course of medication? If the answer is yes, just walk away.

4 Interrogate dating agency personnel unremittingly. Are they themselves happily married? Did they meet through an agency? If not, why not? What makes them so different? Don't they feel dating agencies are good enough for them? Leave no stone unturned, she will either throw her arms up in the air and admit that her business is fraudulent or say the real reason you're single is because you're such an irritating nosy cow.

*I love your rippling muscles,
I love your eyes so blue,
I feel your arms around me
As you promise to be true.*

*My darling Stevie,
my cuddly teddy bear,
I want to hide under
the sheets with you —
forever...*

A GUIDE TO PLASTIC SURGERY

Now that you've finally found your dream lover, you want to look perfect for him forever. Unfortunately life is not like that and before you can say HRT, your bosoms will be dragging on the floor and your skin will be as wrinkly as lizards. But that is precisely why God invented cosmetic surgery.

Film stars and ageing rich women swear by it. Joan Collins is living proof, a nip here, a tuck there and who'd suspect she had first hand memories of the *Titanic*. To all the world and anyone who doesn't get up too close she is young and beautiful.

LOVE

But does cosmetic surgery keep love alive? Who knows? But it certainly keeps it alert. Haven't we all heard the tales of husbands returning from the office in a state of utter confusion. Where is the flat chested, saggy-bottomed old prune he air-kissed goodbye to this morning? And who is that pert, inflatable dolly peeling the potatoes and grinning like a Stepford wife? Why, yes it is none other than his missus after Doctor Miracle has given her a good going over.

GODDESS

Then there is the goddess of plastic surgery herself, Miss Pamela Anderson. Women all over America are being snipped, sliced, tucked and pumped full of silicone. Everyone wants to look like Pammie, the living embodiment of the Barbie doll. But Barbie is not an ideal role model for the modern woman; let's not forget Barbie's somewhat complicated love-life. She has, after all, been in a long-term relationship with Ken who hasn't any genitals, but neither has Barbie, so she doesn't really know what she's missing. Who wants to look like Barbie anyway? Her plain cousin Midge (discontinued back in 1968 due to poor sales) was more of a real woman. Brunette, flat chested, covered in freckles, unlucky in love but at least she had a sense of humour.

Some women can get addicted to plastic surgery, self-help groups have sprouted up all over the United States. It may all start as an effort to put a bit of romance and mystery back into relationships but after seventy-eight operations these women have become junkies. "NEVER AGAIN" they shriek, but they can't help it. They leave the house to do the weekly shop and come back with a new pair of tits.

HOW MUCH?

Gone are the days when a depressed woman rushes out to buy a new hat, now she just gets a new head. But let's examine the cost.

These little transformations don't come cheap and unless you can come up with a pretty good psychological life threatening reason why they should be carried out, they don't come on the NHS.

Women everywhere are trotting about proudly with fleshy slices of their thigh grafted on their chins and why not? They smile slyly as their husbands nibble their taut dainty necks. Would he still do it if he knew where that neck used to be? We doubt it. Call us old fashioned but we think it's polite to keep heads and tails as far apart as is humanly possible.

Ideally your husband or lover should pay the bill, you are doing it for him after all (or so you tell him). Obviously once you've had everything fixed you'll look so gorgeous that no man will be able to resist you. Naturally you'll fall in love with someone else who's much better looking and likes you just the way you are. Ex-spouses may get half of everything but no matter how tenacious your husband's solicitors are – even *they* can't demand you have your operations reversed or give your hubby one of your new boobies.

One man longed for a wife just like his mom, so he had a plastic surgeon remodel his girlfriend to resemble his deceased mother. After twenty-nine painful operations and four years of recuperation his fiancée was a dead ringer for his old mum. Love blossomed, they married but then soon divorced because even in mom's old apron she still couldn't make an apple pie just the way he liked it. According to legend, Patsy Kensit ordered a bum tuck before her second wedding, which is really taking the "something old, something new, something borrowed, something blue" wisdom a bit too far. The reception was a disaster as poor Patsy couldn't sit down without splitting her stitches and let's face it, Patsy standing up is not a good idea as it only gives her a

Unfortunately this is not the same as buying a bra – you can't try them on first. Some boob jobs can go horribly wrong – spare a thought for Molly Jerkin who went from a small if not perfectly formed 34AA to a 48D (and that was just the left one).

FOR MEN

Of course cosmetic improvement is not exclusive to women. As we speak, men all over the Western world are perusing penile extension catalogues for something that appeals to them. They are convinced if they buy a bigger willy they'll have more success in pulling the birds. But this is a delicate operation and if not carried out properly they won't even be able to pull the old todger without considerable discomfort. Is it really worth all that agony just so they aren't embarrassed at the urinal? Of course it is.

LEAVING *Love* NOTES

In the early days of your affair, these sweet, soppy, sickly love notes are compulsory. In fact you won't be able to move around the bed without tripping over the scraps of scented paper postscripted with a thousand kisses. When your boyfriend goes to shave in the morning you will have stuck a Post-It Note on the bathroom mirror saying "Do you miss me?" even though he last saw you two minutes earlier and will be seeing you again as soon as he finishes shaving (assuming of course he doesn't melt at the sight of your handwriting and slit his throat with the razor by mistake).

At the height of your love you will attempt your own version of the ghastly 1970s "Love Is" characters who never had to say they were sorry. (Though we sure as hell wish their creator would.)

He depicts you looking cute and pretty and you draw bulging muscles where there are none. This is a unique time in your relationship and one you will definitely want to forget.

After a steamy night of passion the notes can get quite "end of the pier" postcard *risqué*. Hide these notes or better still burn them; it doesn't do to have friends seeing them. Bedroom secrets are just that and no one, no matter how close they are to you, really wants to see a cartoon version of your magnificent naked bosoms and your boyfriend's big pink willie. They'll only laugh at you or quite possibly throw up.

Gradually the novelty of writing romantic notes fades and as the relationship deepens the notes get more pedestrian…

…and the longer you live together the notes will eventually become nasty and downright rude. After a while you'll just stop talking to each other altogether. You'll leave notes or e-mail messages and pretty soon the only time you'll hear your partner's voice will be on the answerphone when they're calling to say they'll be late yet again.

THE NEW LOVERS' FRIDGE

let's have an early night

XXXXX
XXXX
XXX

I want you NOW

theres Haagen Daas in the freezer

don't be cheeky

I'm going to smear it all over your thighs then lick it off!

THE OLD LOVERS' FRIDGE

Who ate my ice cream?

it was *our* ice cream

You don't need it — you're too FAT

sod off you BASTARD!

...ve you.

By the way — shagging your BEST FRIEND

ADVICE ON LOVE AND INFATUATION

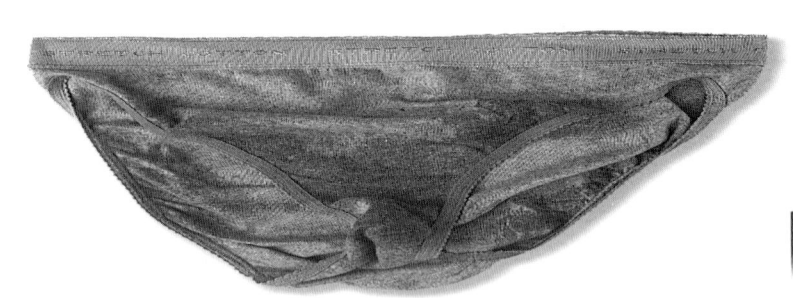

Even though love makes the world go round and is a many splendoured thing, it can also make you behave in peculiar ways.

UNHEALTHY LOVE

It is never a good idea to develop a fixation on a person, particularly if you've never even been introduced to them. Fantasizing about Peter André as your perfect lover and decorating your bedroom walls with pictures of him is one thing, but following him obsessively around the city and waiting on his doorstep night after night, could be termed by law as stalking.

Very naughty! His bodyguards will have you handcuffed, thrown in the cells and given a restraining order before anyone has a chance to say "Mysterious girl, I want to get close to you."

Now we know these days that stalking is quite fashionable, in fact, some film stars have it written into their contracts that a stalker must be provided, as it does quite a lot for their image. But even so, it really is not a good habit to take up. It is a lonely (not to mention dangerous) hobby that will only earn you the nickname of weirdo.

Fan clubs, however, are slightly more acceptable, but those too attract their fair share of nutters.

A BRIEF HISTORY OF FAN WORSHIP

Back in the 1920s women fell passionately in love with Rudolph Valentino – he was the original Latin lover. When he died more people turned out to watch his funeral procession than were killed in World War I and the majority of the mourners were female. They wanted him – dead or alive.

In the 1960s Beatlemania overtook the world. Sodden panties were tossed on stage and Paul McCartney developed a life-long repulsion for Marks & Spencer's frilly knickers and quite possibly a lifetime devotion to vegetarian food.

The 1980s spawned the monsters known as the Mannilovers. These were (and sadly still are) the fans of Barry Manilow – the sexless unattractive middle-aged singer with a hooter that rivals a horizontal

Canary Wharf Tower in length. But still his fan clubs boast more women per square foot than can be found at a "six for the price of one" Top Shop sale.

Tragically in the 1990s the young are equally guilty of fan club nutterdom. Look how many young girls tried to kill themselves on hearing that Take That had split up! It's one thing to lay down your life for someone who loves you madly and is prepared to do the same thing for you, but it's quite another to try and top yourself just because five lads with funny haircuts decided they can't bear to be in the same room together. Get a grip, these blokes are in it for the money – they did not write "A Million Love Songs" with you in mind.

UNREQUITED LOVE – THE SAD AND BITTER TRUTH:

Infatuation and having a crush on someone can be a beautiful experience. However if it is all one-sided all of the time, watch out. Remember Glenn Close in *Fatal Attraction* – the woman was obviously seriously demented to have found Michael Douglas desirable in the first place, let alone worth boiling a bunny over. (Especially if you're not going to stick around and have a stab at Delia Smith's Traditional English Rabbit Pie ideally with 4 oz of pitted prunes and 10 fl oz of dry cider.)

Just because you share a wonderful one night stand with some gorgeous hunk, it does not mean they want to ever see you again. Sad but true.

THE SIGNS

If you are prone to unrequited love, the signs will emerge quite early on. Think back – at primary school, for example, was there a cute boy who sat behind you but never spoke to you? Did he sometimes rest his feet on your chair causing a thrill of pre-pubescent sexual excitement to course through your tiny underdeveloped body? Did you whittle his name into the desk and scribble it all over your pencil case or, worse still, did you carve his name on to your thigh, where it still remains – a faint white outline that if you look closely says "Mark & Jane 4 Ever"? Yes, there are many signs that will indicate you are an "unrequity". For example: are you convinced the bloke selling tickets at the tube station is in love with you just because he said: "Sorry, I've only got pound coins. You don't mind do you?"?

It is extremely important to know the rules of love and infatuation – the following advice should be heeded at all times:

Don't hide at the bus shelter and follow him home. If he ain't interested, forget him and find somebody else who is. You don't want to end up sad and dejected on some afternoon talk show. This isn't America, no one thinks you're famous just because you've appeared on national television and sobbed your heart out. This is Britain and if you do that, you will be ostracized from society and forced to shop a very long way from your neighbourhood.

Don't phone them twenty-five times a day just to hear their dial tone or answerphone message, then hang up if they do answer in person. This is a very annoying thing to do to someone and can make them very nervous indeed.

Don't take photos of them when they aren't looking and then put the results under your pillow at night. This action is similar to voodoo or witchcraft and will be perceived as such if you dare to confide your loony doings to anyone. Their reaction will only serve to remind you that you are completely barmy.

If you haven't got the guts to tell your admirer how you feel, then don't tell anyone else. Remember, men like to do all the chasing – they are very stupid and need to feel in control at all times.

The way to snare your bloke is to appear totally uninterested. Look gorgeous at all times and when he notices you, ignore him. It's a very childish and evil game but you will definitely attract a more positive response than by posting a pair of your dirty knickers to him and enclosing your phone number.

N.B. If you are victim of a male version of the above, be afraid, be very afraid. (Especially if he still lives with his mother.)

girl*power*

TIPS ON LOVE AND SEDUCTION

The more cynical among us believe that seduction from a woman's point of view is not really necessary. Let's face it, if you lie down naked next to any man, we all know what he's likely to do. But let's pretend there is such a thing and if there is, then let's get it right.

They say a way to a man's heart is through his stomach, which implies that the most important thing to a man is good food. WRONG. If this was true then why would a night out with his mates to the pub, winding up with a mutton vindaloo in a cheap curry house hold so much appeal.

Men don't care what they put inside them as long as it keeps them going. You can spend four hours peeling a radish, then sculpting it into the perfect cupid to garnish a glorious meal that took all day to prepare and will he notice? We doubt it. They don't care what they eat as long as it's dead and doesn't come in blue. Then again, the old swallowing a live goldfish is still a very popular party trick, so we had better discount the "must be dead" theory. If you're setting out to seduce your lover then forget cooking – this is why Marks & Spencer was invented. Pop in an oven-ready and set about your artful seduction.

USEFUL TIPS

The only thing men like more than talking about themselves, is hearing a woman they fancy talking about them too. Make sure that you enquire lovingly about their day at the office and always take their side when they complain about a colleague. Give them your undivided attention and show enthralled interest in everything they have to say but, whatever you do, don't offer any of your own opinions – this will only make them cross and remind them that you are intelligent and have a brain.

1

Always agree with them. They have had a hard day and need to know they have an ally on home turf. If it's pouring with rain and they suggest a walk because it looks like it's about to clear up, go along with it. Don't take an umbrella as they will only see that as your way of knowing better than them. Wellington boots and raincoats are acceptable walking accessories, but don't suggest them, just leave them out where he can see them and hopefully he'll take the hint. If it doesn't clear up, under no circumstances say "I told you so",

2

this will make his male organ shrink and he'll never forgive you for being right.

3 Compliment him constantly. Tell him he looks very handsome and that his new shirt suits him. If he's just had his hair cut and it looks awful then lie – say how trendy it is and how much like Johnny Depp he now looks. If he gives any sign of being insecure about the Johnny Depp remark, then reassure him by saying how much better looking than Johnny Depp he is and how you don't know what anyone sees in Johnny Depp anyway. If he believes this he'll probably believe in alien abduction, which is always a handy excuse for getting out of a date.

4 If he likes sport but is absolutely hopeless at it, then keep it a secret from him. Attend all his weekend footie and rugger matches and cheer relentlessly. Video the game then quickly take it to a special effects editor who can work magic by making your poor boyfriend look much better than he really is. Possibly by superimposing Alan Shearer or Tony Underwood where appropriate.

Wear something stunning and revealing to the games, but cover up with a mac when talking to the other guys. He might assume that all your effort is for the bloke who actually did manage to score and he'll punish you by falling asleep in bed snoring and sweating alcohol.

5 Always let him drive, even if you are a driving instructor and he hasn't passed his test yet. If you drive and you drive better than he does, he will not only hate you but his feeling of inadequacy will probably make him impotent for the rest of your life together. Don't sigh as he overtakes on a blind corner or feebly point to an oncoming vehicle just feet away – that will only be deemed as taking the initiative and God forbid that that should ever happen. He is the man after all and therefore no doubt taller, so naturally his feet reach the pedals more easily than yours and what the hell would you know about driving anyway (you're a woman for God's sake).

6 Offer to give him a massage. Tell him he looks tired and could do with the relaxation. But don't ever let him think you have a sexual motive – this will put the pressure on him and instead of succumbing to your magical hands he will lie there tense and furious that you might arouse him before he had the idea in the first place.

7 If you want your garden landscaped don't ask him outright to do it. Tell him a racy story about a friend of a friend who hired a young stud to do her digging. Describe your friend's lust when taking him a tray of lemonade and Hobnobs and seeing his naked torso gleaming in the sun. Tell him about the adjacent shed complete with rakes, shovels and a fold-out divan. Tell him that the young gardener comes twice a week to do her weeding and often stays till sundown. Add that he is quite reasonable at six pounds an hour and your bulbs aren't blooming as well as they could be. He will not be able to bear the thought of you calling said gardener and will not only shag you senseless, but will no doubt do the gardening every weekend.

girlpower

HISTORY LESSONS IN LOVE

Here we are on the eve of the millennium and have we learned anything? Not a jot. We keep on making the same old mistakes over and over again, so we think it's time we looked back in anger at romances past. Fact and fiction, Kings and Queens, in fact The Good, The Bad and The Fergies.

ROMEO AND JULIET

In our opinion fourteen is far too young to get seriously involved with a boy and actually kill yourself over him. That's just very very silly. At fourteen you should be playing with your Barbies, wetting yourself over Mark Owen and watching *Hollyoaks*, not setting up secret meetings with boys via dodgy vicars and waking up in crypts next to your dead boyfriend and all his smelly old relatives. Mind you, that was then and this is now.

In those days most people's life expectancy was thirty-five which was actually not a bad thing because no one ever had to worry about turning forty and going on HRT.

SCARLETT AND RHETT

Who could forget that emerald-eyed vixen Scarlett O'Hara? Flouncing down the stairs in her pudding shaped crinoline or falling to her knees, clinging on to a carrot crying "As God is my witness, I'll never go hungry again". Liar, if she wasn't hungry how the hell did she still have a sixteen-inch waist after giving birth. But Rhett, on the other hand, was a debonair, moustache-twirling charmer who knew what he wanted and where to get it (he just didn't count on there being so many petticoats in his way). Scarlett's big problem in love was that she didn't know a good thing when she saw it. There she was married to gorgeous Rhett and pining away for weedy old happily married Ashley. She was haunted nightly by the same dream, she was running, running, always running through the woods, through the mist, running towards an unknown man, a handsome man with a moustache and a way with women. "What did it mean?" She'd cry in torment. It was only after good old Rhett left her for the final time, that it dawned on her: "Derrrr, it was Rhett in my dream. Oh no, oh well I'll think about it tomorrow." Dozy cow.

JOHN AND YOKO

The iconoclastic hippie couple of the century. They met at one of Yoko's art shows (and we use the word "art" loosely). Apparently Yoko was exhibiting a fascinating piece called "hammer & nail". John, gobsmacked at what he saw (let's face it they were in Bond Street not on a Wimpey building site) jokingly asked her if he could hammer in a nail. "That will cost you," she replied. He winked and uttered the magic words, "Could I hammer in an imaginary nail then?" Apparently Yoko was so impressed by this visionary riposte she fell in love with him at once and insisted that they sit naked on a bed in an hotel in Amsterdam all in the name of peace. He agreed and surprisingly the war in Vietnam continued and the fall of Saigon was not prevented.

ROD STEWART AND ANY BLONDE

Rod Stewart is as ugly as sin, but for some reason (possibly his giant bank account) he is a blonde magnet. We personally believe the only reason he marries blondes is because he has a terrible memory for names, and being the sort of cad he is, he's destined to be with more than one woman. So, logically if he nicknames his beloved "blondie", then that's all he need remember. Do you think I'm sexy? No Rod, we think you're sixty – you're very old and very rich – so who needs sexy?

QUEEN VICTORIA

Queen Victoria was not a pretty woman but she was well respected and managed to put her name to an entire era. Think of Queen Victoria and think of the chimney-sweep children, people dying of consumption and a world without sex. She was besotted with her only husband Albert: a fat man with a long moustache and a lot of hair. Though fond of her, and father to her many children, he simply couldn't keep it in his trousers. As Vicky was so often pregnant he had no choice but to "put it about" all over town. She knew of this but loved him anyway – she never divorced him and mourned him forever when he died. Or did she? Perhaps she only stayed with him so that a certain London museum could have a decent name. For all his sins, the Victoria & Albert Museum is a pretty catchy name.

CLEOPATRA

Cleopatra was the woman who had it all: looks, brains and a large part of Africa. Named after jazz singing legend Cleo Laine, she was the most desirable woman in the world. How could she find a bloke to be her match? Hardly down the pub. No, she doffed her cap and much else to Julius Caesar, the man who owned most of the rest of the world. A match made in heaven, apart, that is of course due to his wife and the hostility of the Senate. After Caesar was murdered by his friends during a bit of rough and tumble that got out of hand (Friday nights are always a bit rowdy in decadent empires), Cleopatra opted for love, this time with Mark Antony, who had accidently got two first names and no surname which meant he couldn't be emperor. But this didn't matter as she was willing to share everything with him. He, however, believed that men should be the breadwinners and started going out and getting into trouble with his old mates. It didn't work out in the end but Cleopatra was just a bit ahead of her time – a very very early feminist, so well done to her.

LIZ TAYLOR

The most beautiful woman that has ever lived. Liz Taylor has had eight marriages. Talk about hedging your bets. This did mean though that she had some very eligible men and of course some ineligible e.g. Eddie Fisher who was Debbie Reynolds' husband at the time. However, her husband's desertion has provided Debbie with a whole new career as a cabaret star and cuckold. Liz, on the other hand, seems to have wisely given up men in favour of charity, perfume and Michael Jackson.

QUEEN ELIZABETH I

Unlike her namesake above, Elizabeth the Queen of England, who reigned over the discovery of fags and chips, never had any blokes at all, according to historians. As all these historians were men and it was the 17th century, we will draw a veil over this one, imagining that in reality Liz had a very good time indeed as befits a woman in her position. The Virgin Queen – we don't think so.

girlpower

THE DO'S AND DON'TS OF LOVE ON YOUR HONEYMOON

Honeymoon is in itself an odd yet evocative word. The Oxford dictionary defines it as "The initial period of ardour or enthusiasm". Break the words up and you have: honey… a sweet viscid yellow fluid, and moon…a monthly satellite that revolves around the Earth. Put these two definitions together in relation to a newly-wed couple and they make no sense whatsoever. Nonetheless, here are a few of our tips to surviving a honeymoon.

It doesn't matter where you go, people will know you are on your honeymoon. They can smell it and we mean that in the nicest possible way. The clues are obvious.

MOST POPULAR TELL-TALE SIGNS OF HONEYMOONERS

- You're both wearing wedding bands but you have no children.
- You're still talking to each other and you display affection in public.
- He is constantly complimenting you on your looks. You can't walk straight from endless nights of passion and have developed cystitis, the honeymooner disease, and yet still you walk around with a smile on your face.
- He offers to paint natural yoghurt on your raw parts and you giggle in tender anticipation.
- You call each other pathetic nicknames – fluffy button, baby face, pooky poo, Mr Toot, kitten pie etc. and everyone else at the holiday resort hates you.
- You also feel tempted to spoon feed each other in restaurants, licking bits of drooling sauce off your chins. You eat in bed and dive for crumbs that have landed in out of the way places and you commit every deviant sexual act in the book *Deviant Sexual Acts Made Easy* but you still have the good manners not to pass wind in front of each other.
- You excuse yourself when you belch and giggle in a mock shocked way as if to say "…my goodness, who'd have thought me capable".

You are still in love so enjoy… because just about everything you've experienced on your honeymoon will seem so gross and disgusting in years to come that you'll wonder why you weren't arrested.

ADVICE TO HONEYMOONERS

Don't team up with another newly-wed couple. You'll only get all competitive in trying to prove which couple is the most in love or worse still you'll all get so drunk and happy that you'll imagine an intimacy between you that doesn't really exist. This may lead to group sex and the dread of ever running into each other again. Disasterous if you're all staying on a tiny Caribbean island with one departing charter flight per month.

Be careful because you're not safe on your own either. You will take embarrassing photos of each other in ludicrous positions, probably naked and mooning in the shower. If these shots do get developed and not confiscated, please, please destroy them because you will have believed him when he said "don't worry, how on earth will anyone ever know that's you". Take our word for it – they will. Especially when he takes his prize photo to work and places it on his desk. You'll meet him in the pub afterwards and his colleagues will snigger and blush then finally after a few drinks casually pay you compliments like "nice beaver" then look painfully embarrassed and mutter "sorry, I meant briefcase, yeah you've got a nice briefcase there, really like the way it opens".

Don't be tempted to take a camcorder with you. Videos are a terrible mistake. Don't pose for anything that can be fast forwarded or freeze framed. You don't want to end up the star of some dodgy home-made porn flick that fetches three quid on the market or worse still make an appearance on *You've Been Framed*.

If you have had a terrible time you may return with a sense of relief, thinking you don't have to go all through that again – but for some, the nightmare returns in…

THE SECOND HONEYMOON

This phenomenon occurs for various reasons. One of these is that a married couple have been together happily for many years and are still madly in love and feel they wish to take their vows again and go on another honeymoon, sometimes they return to the place they visited some thirty years earlier. Very romantic, if not sick-making.

Another common reason for the second honeymoon syndrome is when one of the pair feels guilty. This is probably due to an extramarital affair. They hope they can make up for all that hurt and pain by taking their wounded spouse somewhere gorgeous and spending a fortune on them. If this happens, it's always wise to assume this will help restore relations, but don't stop on the second. Insist on a third, fourth or however many it takes to get over the dreadful betrayal.

POPULAR HONEYMOON DESTINATIONS

Mauritius and The Seychelles are the most sought after hot spots. Followed by Paris, Switzerland, Barbados or a world cruise. The latter is not really a good idea, let's face it, if you end up having an enormous row it's very awkward to swim back home.

Horror honeymoons vary from the delights of staying the night in a B&B in Solihull to a Civil War re-creation weekend.

Going anywhere with your in-laws or his best friend is a big no no. You have just started out on your married life and you don't really want to spend the first twenty-five years in a closed prison, which may happen if you get a bit tense and resort to murdering a member of his family.

HOW TO DEAL WITH LOVE AND HYGIENE

OR HOW IMPORTANT IS THE "H"-WORD IN KEEPING LOVE ON THE BOIL?

Your eyes meet across a crowded club. He looks like Johnny Depp and you look like Kate Moss. You flirt, you chat, you snog each other's faces off. Attraction rules and it sure smells sweet.

Cut to three months' dating later. Your boyfriend makes to tangle lips with you but that burger-breath puts you right off. In a tight clinch you can't help noticing BO buzzing and sweat patches on his Oasis T-shirt. Meanwhile he clocks that there's enough wax in your shell-like to make a hippy candle.

In the excitement of action-packed first love, hygiene doesn't loom large, but familiarity breeds contempt. In the bright light of day, when everyone's slacked off making an effort, you start to notice those gnawing details. Suddenly it's not his twinkly smile that catches your eye, but the spinach caught between his teeth.

ADVICE FOR YOU AND FOR HIM

When it comes to staying sexy, the body is a minefield. Top danger areas include bad breath (avoid garlic, onions and alcohol), grubby ears, dirty nails (especially when long), slimy hair, cheesy feet (air those post-club trainers), unsavoury X-rated bits (guys get that soap out!), sweaty underarms, too much hair (get hip to shaving, people!), smelly clothes (watch that tomato sauce and white T-shirt combo) and smoky fumes (lose that Marlboro habit).

Right up there with bad body control are sloppy habits. Hygiene isn't just about brushing your teeth ten times a day and hanging out at the local launderette looking for the perfect partner – it's about not being a slob.

YOUR PERSONAL HYGIENE

It's no good dressing in Prada if your room looks like a parrot's cage. Similarly why wow someone with your flower-fresh breath, if you pick your teeth in a revolting way and guzzle leftovers off your lover's plate without asking (before licking your own)?

girl*power*

If it is you who is the hygiene horror then it's easy enough to smarten up your act. But what's a girl to do when her boyfriend exhibits the above symptoms? Lump him or dump him? It's one thing if your man is scruffy in a cool, blokey way, but if going in for a close-up leaves you gagging for air then he's taken rough 'n' ready styling a tad too far.

HIS PERSONAL HYGIENE

To keep passion in fashion in a long-term relationship, cleanliness is vital, so tell your fella if he's turning you off. It's embarrassing to mention straight out that someone's got dandruff, so go for more subtle hint-dropping. Give him some ace shampoo as a present (if he's bright he'll get the message), or flatter him with some ego-boosting lines "Hey, love that shirt" and then follow up with a more craftily phrased criticism "You know, you'd be even sexier if you looked after your skin a little more".

If your lover's just got mild hygiene flaws he'll take the hint, but if he's an out-and-out tramp he may need more serious bribery. Try the dangling the carrot from a stick approach. Offer him more nookie, nice nights out and naughtiness if he takes a shower and less if he won't. It's amazing how fast some men come around.

WHEN SCRUFFY IS SEXY

Stephen Dorff **Keanu Reeves** **Jarvis Cocker**

WHEN CLEAN IS MEAN

David Duchovny **David Ginola** **Richard Gere**

girl*power*

LOVE IS FULL OF *Surprises*

Spontaneity is the fizz that gives your love whizz.

Remember those heady days of dating back in month one? When you used to give your man a giant snog just when he least expected it. Remember the way he used to take you out on mystery dates to the beach (or suddenly present you with some killer MAC lippie and a Kookaï frock out of the blue). Everything was so fun, so unpredictable, so romantic and new.

But when that first rush of "in-love" good times has shot by, it's easy to fall into a "warm mules by the fire" type of relationship. "Mr-Pulse-Racingly-Gorgeous" starts to look (and act) more and more like a faithful hound – loyal, dependable and friendly, but hardly raunch on legs. Meanwhile, you start to feel more and more like a 1950s wifey cooing "Hi honey, how was your day?" when "Mr-Getting-Boring-Now" picks you up for a date; and nagging him over his choice of clothes (the very same ones you used to love him for).

So just how do you ensure your love stays a wild child? As any battle commander knows, the key to winning is the element of surprise. Spring a cool gift or shocking new date idea on your lover and he'll know you still find him sexy and exciting. What's more you'll actually feel sexy and exciting too.

Having a routine is indeed a sign of intimacy and cosiness, but it can suck a big one in terms of rocking romance. Keep things happening by suggesting spontaneous things to do. But ditch obvious clichés like a fancy dinner or a bunch of flowers.

Instead, make up your own customized version of romance. Take your bloke to the zoo or on a date to an aquarium – it'll bring out the animal in him for sure. Go for a Chinese takeaway in the park at sunset and drink low-budget wine. Spend a weekend watching six movies back-to-back in the cinema. Check out the dinosaurs in the Natural History Museum. Take him on a mystery date, even if it's just a slap-up meal down the local caff and his choice of video at home afterwards.

Make sure the stuff you do feels totally new. If you usually slob out at weekends by the telly, take him to an art gallery or a football match. If you usually shop till you drop and club till dawn, try staying in bed with magazines and popcorn.

Presents are another wicked way to make your bloke feel special, but again don't just go for the obvious (chocs) or the expensive (even bigger box of chocs). Dumb stuff that's tacky or kitsch can be more of a laugh than a flash meal out (that *Star Wars* figure or indoor firework for instance). Pick something that shows you really know your man (the CD he mentioned he wanted three months ago cause it's the thought and imagination that counts.

Remember it's not just what you give, but when, where and how. It's the unprompted out-of-season little somethings that'll really stick in his mind. Even if your gift is a small one, careful packaging or a well-chosen spot to deliver it at a special time will go just as far to win his heart (like hiding lots of little presents inside a cool record bag to take him off his guard).

Holidays are another sexy way to keep your love humming. Whether it's a weekend in Amsterdam or a day-trip to Brighton, travel is great because you both let down your hair and let unsuspected sides of your personalities out of the bag.

The smallest things you do matter too. Like that amazing moment when your man offers to brush your hair. Or when you suddenly kiss his eyebrow or slowdance in the living-room.

But remember, you cannot force surprise culture on unwilling victims. How many guys do you know who've been about to make a surprise phone call to their girl to say "I love you" when she's rung him first and chewed off his ear? Give your man space to pick his own moments in his own way – one guy's romance meat is another's love poison.

FIVE SURPRISES HE'LL MARRY YOU FOR

- catching you in bed (clutching a picture of him)
- dirty phone calls from yours truly while he's at work
- new lingerie on a regular basis
- discovering you're not afraid of sex toys
- finding out you've hired a cleaner

FIVE SURPRISES HE WON'T THANK YOU FOR

- catching you in bed (with another guy)
- finding you've been phoning Oz – on his mobile
- a wedding proposal (after your first date)
- you're pregnant (and it's his)
- you're pregnant (and it isn't)

FIRST LOVE NEVER DIES

HOW TO DEAL WITH FIRST LOVE HIGHS AND FIRST SPLIT BLUES…

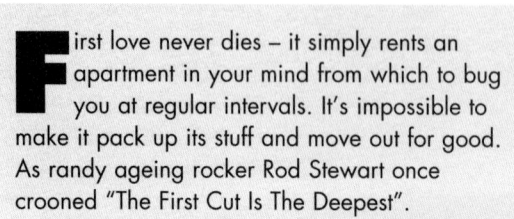

First love never dies – it simply rents an apartment in your mind from which to bug you at regular intervals. It's impossible to make it pack up its stuff and move out for good. As randy ageing rocker Rod Stewart once crooned "The First Cut Is The Deepest".

The first time you fall for someone is better than sex, better than an outsize bar of chocolate and even beats dinner *à deux* with the pop star of your choice. The Big Love Thing is what everyone in the world is waiting for – and five billion punters can't be wrong.

First love turns you into a shiny happy person overnight. Suddenly you don't care if it's raining. You'll catch yourself yelling, "have a nice day!" at total strangers. Your phone bill will grow bigger than the Empire State Building and you'll notice that every relationship song or poem seems to be written just for you. Basically it's like living on another planet, 'cause the world inside your head starts turning the real one upside down.

But first love can be hotter to handle than the sand on *Baywatch* beach. Your new lover snaffles the emotional slot your parents, friends, demanding 1990s job, CD collection and designer Dalmatian used to fill. Dealing with a new wave of heavy duty emotions can leave you feeling freaked out and insecure. It's a bit like giving the keys of your new Ford Fiesta to a joyrider.

Sure you'll probably feel "luvved up", but fucked up is often the flipside of the card. It's easy to get clingy, dependent, possessive, jealous or just plain passive when "Dreamboy Number One" enters your life.

TELL-TALE SIGNS OF MELTDOWN INCLUDE

- stalking him
- 1471-ing all your unidentified calls in case he's got a secret girlfriend (ditto last number redial if he's just been on the dog and bone)
- having his name tattooed on your butt (this will date quicker than flares)
- agreeing to cook and wash up for him and fifteen mates while they watch the footie
- crying when he goes away (and most of the time when he's with you too)
- dressing as a French maid just to please him and allowing him to take photos

You never fall further than from the dizzy heights of first love. Especially if you've been dumped, it's like someone's pulled a cosy rug out from under your feet. One minute your future was chock full of "that special person" but the next you're left depressed on your own, endlessly spinning "your song". The bastard has decided to swap drying your tears for causing them!

girl*power*

Okay so it's hard to believe that future loves mean forever, when you've seen "Mr Right" turn into "Mr Right Git" in front of your eyes. First love makes a mega impression and marks you with its dating style so strongly that other ways of doing things seem alien (for instance your ex liked going clubbing, but your new boy prefers to slack at home by the telly). But most of us would trade that "first time around" card for experience any day.

On the plus side, future relationships are often much funkier and less uptight, because you know the rules of the game and can learn from past mistakes. Okay so you may lose that wide-eyed innocence ("Jamie is God, plays guitar better than Oasis and we're going to get married!"), but you'll be more clued up about new love encounters.

How many of us assume our first boyfriend is hotter in bed than Don Juan only to find out that "boyfriend three" makes him look more cack-handed than Edward Scissorhands? It's easier to define the limits of boyfriend behaviour, say, fourth time around, because you'll have other examples to compare your "Loverman" to.

It can take years to see your first lover's faults for what they were (and finish compiling your hate diary to the berk!). After all, the way old Dougy hogged the mirror probably worked up your nerves big-time! Not to mention the way he thought turning up at your place pissed, late, stinking of fags and semi-conscious counted as a turn-on. Or that two-timing you with your best friend would somehow bring you all closer! In fact, looking back, the guy was probably a bigger fashion mistake than Nigel from *EastEnders* and more of a tosser than Hugh Grant.

Sure, keep a place in your heart for the first guy who broke it, but don't let past love paralyze your life. You've got to move on and groove on (with your girlfriends' help), because the most important relationship you'll ever have is with yourself. So just look after number one.

girl*power*

MISTAKING LOVE WITH FRIENDSHIP

This may sound like a contradiction and we don't mean going with your gay friends to a nightclub and dancing until three without once being hit on (bliss). What we mean is the usually teenage syndrome of having what you think is a romance, with a gay man. You meet him at school or college, he's attractive, he's sensitive and he talks to women like they are human beings (a skill most straight men don't acquire until much later in life, if at all).

You develop a huge crush, he seems so much more mature than the other boys in your class and doesn't want to join in with their macho competitive bragging. Finally he asks you out. You go to see a film with River Phoenix in it. In the cinema you notice that he seems to be at least as genuinely interested in the film as you are (and especially the bits with River in them) and he doesn't try to snog you once. How charming, you think, what a gentleman…

Years later you bump into him in your local supermarket; he invites you to dinner, telling you to bring your boyfriend. You are puzzled until he adds, "You can meet my new man, he's lovely." Now it all slots into place. The weeks of going to parties where he was more interested in dancing than helping you lose your virginity (which as we all know is the real motive behind teenage parties), his ability to see women as people rather than sex objects, his tendency to have a few good friends rather than be one of the macho "gang".

The youthful experience of this phenomenon is the most usual and can be seen, at least in retrospect as the means of gaining a great friend, rather than that of losing a boyfriend. Thankfully we live in a society that makes it possible for most young gay men and lesbians to "come out" before they are too old.

However, there are cases when, due to family or work pressures, the person feels they have to at least put in an appearance of heterosexuality well into later life. This can lead to heartache, not only for them, but also for the girlfriends or even wives involved.

girl*power*

THE POP STAR'S/ POLITICIAN'S "BEARD"

We've all had that conversation over a drink down at the local. One of your mates who knows someone who works for a newspaper says that they know for a fact that so-and-so (a public figure) is gay. But, you say, he/she is married. "Since when did that mean anything?" is the cynical yet accurate response to that question.

If you end up dating a guy who is using you as a "badge" to prove he is straight, it's not as easy as you might think to spot that his preferences lie elsewhere. All the clichés about gay men, how they dress, speak and behave, are simply not true. He might even overcompensate by behaving in a more-macho-than-thou manner, getting into too many fights and chatting up women compulsively. Obviously, if he feels he has something to hide he will probably over-react if any suggestion is made that he is anything other than a hetero-guy (think suing newspapers or photo-shoots of happy families), which may be the only hint that you will detect of his real nature.

It's probably best to avoid the company of politicians and spoilt pop stars and if one of their number do ask you out, only accept if you are an out-of-work actress in need of publicity.

I CAN CHANGE HIM

No, no, no. Some women fall in love with men that they know with their head to be gay, but in their stupid heart think that they can, through the power of their love, utterly transform. It's like a grotesque distortion of a Country song or romantic fiction gone wrong.

"As Miranda implored Bradley, her breast heaved with passion. 'What have I been missing out on all this time?' He thought and kissed her. In the distance waves crashed on to a moonlit shore. Blah, blah, blah."

If you meet a gay man who is attractive and amusing, realize that you have met a new friend. It is permissible to ask if he has a brother who is straight and up for grabs only once you know him very well (it's good manners). No self-respecting girl should waste her life waiting for the impossible, you might as well decide to hold your breath until there is a 100 per cent reliable contraceptive. Actually, falling in love with a gay man might be it.

BISEXUAL

Not really much different from going out with a straight man. Either you can trust him to be faithful or you can't. The fact that he finds both sexes attractive means only if he does cheat on you, you'll discover it's just as upsetting whatever his choice. The only difference is that you say "hands off" to both your sister and your brother when you first take him home to meet your family.

A Guide to Lovey Dovey Presents

Love and presents go together like fish and chips, especially when you're in that soppy early stage where you want to give him everything, even if you have to pawn all your furniture and blow your credit card limit into the stratosphere. You can't help it – you just want to make him very happy and give him something that reminds him of you.

Unfortunately retailers have caught on to this and produce millions of cutie gifts, which girls lust to buy when they're half-mad with love. Here are some of them.

CUTE & CORNY

TEDDY BEARS, LIONS, DUCKS AND BABY SEALS
All with strokeable fur, sad, little eyes and mournful mouths that seem to say, "Please love me!" These aren't for children (they're into Power Rangers); these are for grown-ups.

STUFFED DOLLS, MUGS, KEYRINGS, UNDERPANTS
All with slogans saying "World's Best Lover", "I (heart) You". Why don't they ever say things like "Look I'm Quite Fond Of You, But Don't Get Too Keen As I'm Not Sure I Want To Settle Into A Serious Monogamous Thing Just Yet".

HEART-SHAPED ANYTHINGS
Just because you're in love it doesn't mean you should feel obliged to buy chocolate hearts, heart cushions, heart cuff-links or heart mobiles, etc.

GINORMOUS PADDED GREETINGS CARDS
They're bigger than your house and a lot more expensive. They have verses like:

*You're the only one for me,
You really are divine,
I'm feeling jolly happy,
Because I've made you mine.
You are my perfect shining knight,
Your armour it does gleam,
You fill my world with golden light,
If you know what I mean.*

If you find this anything less than totally repulsive, you should be locked up. The thing is, there's so little thought in a verse like this (we should know, we wrote it).

REALLY GOOD PRESENTS

For him
- Expensive soft shirts in luscious colours with fine stitching and exquisite buttons
- A case of beers from around the world
- A subscription to his top football/computer/music/film/men's magazine
- A big fluffy bathrobe
- Two tickets for a weekend in Paris
- CDs of all his favourite songs that he doesn't have yet
- That screwdriver/ratchet/pair of pliers that would make his tool-box complete
- A personal taped message that he only finds when he gets in his car after leaving for work
- All the ingredients to his favourite meal, prepared by you, with candles, napkins and a plunging cleavage
- A photo of you looking like a supermodel for his desk.

For you
- A designer dress in your favourite colour (clue: subtle comments to him while you are drooling over the fashion pages)
- A magnum of champagne
- 50 red roses
- A set of sexy silk lingerie
- Two tickets for a weekend in Venice
- A video of *Pretty Woman*, *Brief Encounter* or *Truly, Madly, Deeply*
- State-of-the-art storage jars/wine glasses/fruit bowl/kettle/whisk
- A personal love-message for you to find under your pillow
- A huge bottle of massage lotion to be used by him on you
- A photo of him looking like James Dean for your desk.

And that's enough love for anyone...

Love IN THE FIRST FEW WEEKS OF A RELATIONSHIP

You've had a date or two and your man has scored very highly on the following criteria: facial pleasantness, ability to speak in grammatical sentences, kissing technique, good jokes, and wide-eyed adoration of you. Your next step is to allow yourself the delicious luxury of falling for him – hook, line and sinker. This period in a relationship is the "Magic Time". Cherish it, it is rare and precious and all too soon it will be gone, forgotten in a stonking great barney about whose turn it is to descale the kettle.

This is the time that all the poets and lyricists write about when they're describing falling in love. When Annie Lennox sang, "I walk into an empty room/and suddenly my heart goes boom/there's an orchestra of angels/and they're playing with my heart" she wasn't talking about the feeling you have for someone after twenty-five years of domestic cosiness. No, this is the time of "Fever in the morning and fever all through the night" and "Ooooh I can't control myself/Ooh, I can't control myself/Don't leave me hanging on the telephone".

The first few weeks are the interlude of golden bliss when the two of you can see no flaws in the other, but only magnificent virtues. The way he drives so fast is terribly thrilling, the cheery way he chats to till-girls in Tescos is so sweet, the way he always burns the scrambled eggs only enhances the flavour. There's not a dangerous, disloyal or irritating thing he can do that you won't interpret as a charming eccentricity or a delightful new way of doing things that you hadn't thought of before. The words "rose-tinted" and "spectacles" come to mind.

This is the period when you unearth your past for one another, when you describe your family, ex-partners, assorted jobs and the incredibly funny time you went trampolining at Pontins aged nine, only you'd forgotten you weren't wearing any pants and God you've never been so embarrassed! These stories go on long into the night and bond you closer together, in understanding and appreciation of the past events that have made you the fabulous god-like creatures you are today. Not only are you falling in love with him, you are also falling in love with yourself – you see your effect on him, your own stories seem fascinating, your own, desired, body feels great to you. The two of you are buffing up each others' egos until they shine like mirrors.

How compatible you are! You both watch *Brookside*, you both hate olives, you both have middle names that begin with an "A". It's uncanny! You were obviously meant for each other. (Tragically – love tends to gloss over the serious incompatibilities – he's an Islamic Fundamentalist, you're Jewish; he's a Montague, you're a Capulet.)

In this phase, you can hardly bear to be apart, and when you are, you're thinking of him. Many a bus journey is enlivened by calling up the memory of that sweet hairy mole on his nose or the adorable way he pronounces "Weetabix", or the intimacy of the night when you cut his toenails for the first time and felt deeply privileged.

girl*power*

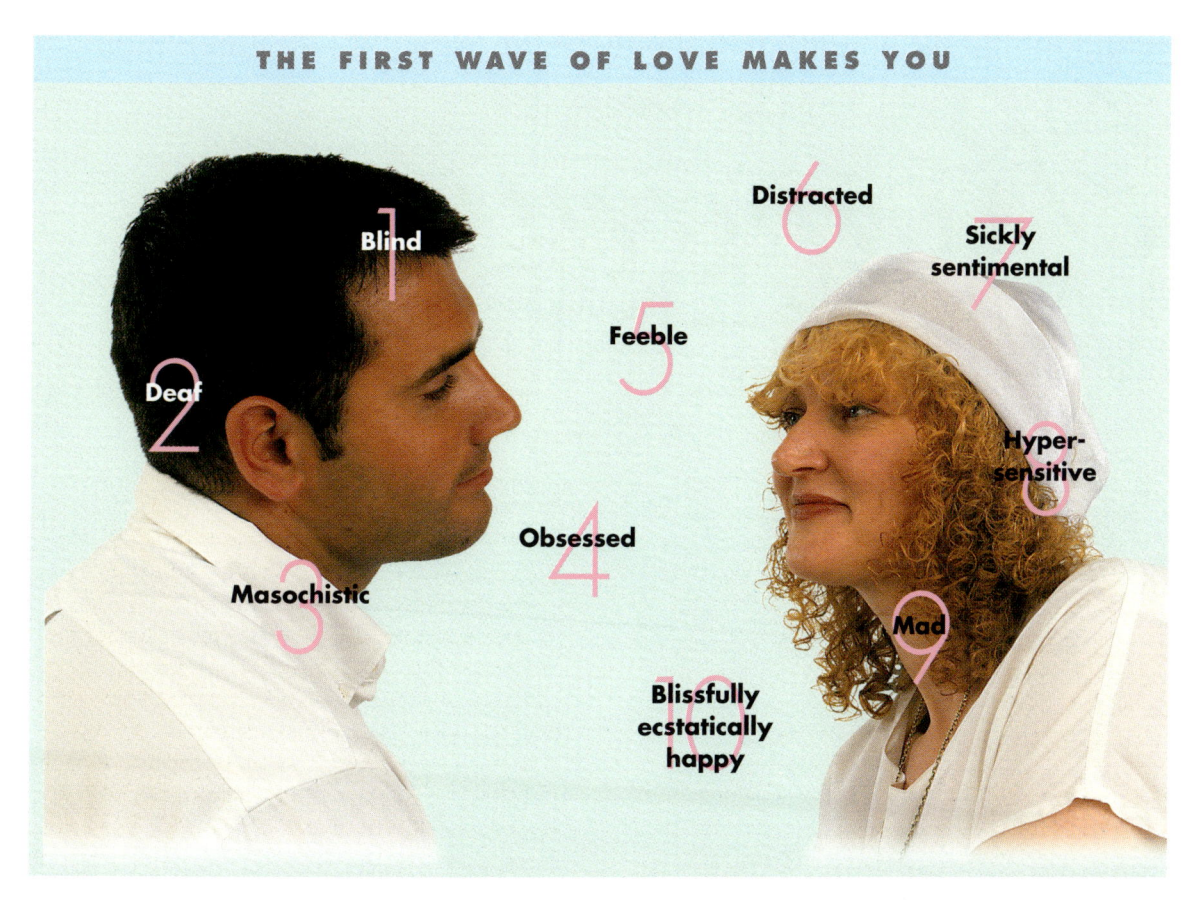

83

THE FIRST WAVE OF LOVE MAKES YOU

1. Blind
2. Deaf
3. Masochistic
4. Obsessed
5. Feeble
6. Distracted
7. Sickly sentimental
8. Hyper-sensitive
9. Mad
10. Blissfully ecstatically happy

TIME-MANAGEMENT IN THE FIRST FEW WEEKS

- 86% In bed
- 3% Walking arm in arm in attractive outdoor locations
- 2% Writing love notes to him
- 4% In candlelit restaurants
- 3% On phone to him
- 1.5% Listening to soppy love songs
- 0.5% Working, shopping, housework, sleeping etc.

The only way that this "Magic Time" will not be spoilt by the inevitable and dreadful intrusion of "Real Life" is if you:

1. Kill yourselves in mutual suicide pact. Er…that's it.

Because (cynical though it sounds) this time will pass – you will come to the end of the hazy, dream-like "First Phase" and discover the things you don't like about each other, at which point you will either split up or decide "It's Worth Working On". If you're very dedicated, you might get a long-term relationship that's more fulfilling than being on your own. But hey! While you're still on Cloud Nine, enjoy! (You'll never get a better high…)

girl*power*

A GUIDE TO *Romantic* WEEKENDS

The occasional romantic or, if you prefer, "dirty" weekend is essential to keep a relationship from going rancid. You need at least two free days, a big bed in a comfortable place, food and drink on tap as desired, and each other.

Just follow these simple tips and we promise you'll feel the benefit.

HOW TO PREPARE

Plan the weekend at least a month in advance – the mere thought of it will give you sustenance when being in love seems to consist mainly of staring blankly at each other over pints of warm lager in the Broom & Bucket.

Do something new to your appearance, like dye your hair blonde or blonder; have a little tattoo done somewhere very personal and don't reveal it until your first night away. Better still – buy yourself a nice posh "going away" hat.

If you have any unresolved tiffs, make a big fat apology to him to clear the air, even if it was all his fault. This is one of the few occasions when it's worth eating humble pie over a row.*

PLACES TO GO

GRAND OLD CASTLES OR
CUTE LITTLE COTTAGES
Must have the picturesque charm of great age, but be cunningly modernized with full central heating, jacuzzi and deep-pile everything. Rent a servant if possible.

PARIS OR VIENNA OR PRAGUE OR VENICE
Some of Europe's most exquisitely beautiful cities – just being there should make you giddy with romantic excitement.
Do stand on lamplit bridges gazing at antique buildings reflected in inky canals.
Don't go on an all-day bus trip round the city with an incomprehensible tour guide and thirty Japanese businessmen.

YOUR OWN BEDROOM
Transformed with drapes, cushions, candles and a crate of champagne into a den of iniquity. Forget real life – just concentrate on weaving two bodies closer together than has ever been thought physically possible.

girl*power*

PLACES TO AVOID

Anywhere that can only be reached via a million teeny weeny roads that all look the same on the map: neither navigator nor driver (nor love) can survive.

Parents' homes either with or without parents. The combination of terrible furnishings, a cocktail cabinet featuring only sweet sherry and horrible childhood memories will kill the most raging passions.

The typical British B&B – stained candlewick bedspreads, plastic tubs of UHT milk, the smell of boiled cabbage, a hideous landlady with brittle permed hair and the smile of a boa constrictor…mmmmm. Feeling sexy?

THINGS TO TAKE

Perfume
Preferably something like Hormone of Deer on Heat and definitely not English Country Garden

Vat of massage lotion

Shockingly sexy underwear
that you'd feel silly wearing at home.

Pro-Plus

Walkman
with two pairs of headphones so you can share a slushy soundtrack

A can of squirty cream

THINGS NOT TO TAKE

Your kids
Your mum
Big knickers
TV guide
Mobile phone
Stout shoes

* **Others are:** Christmas, when you're mountain climbing together and you're attached to his rope, when he's threatening not to buy you that new handbag you wanted until you apologize.

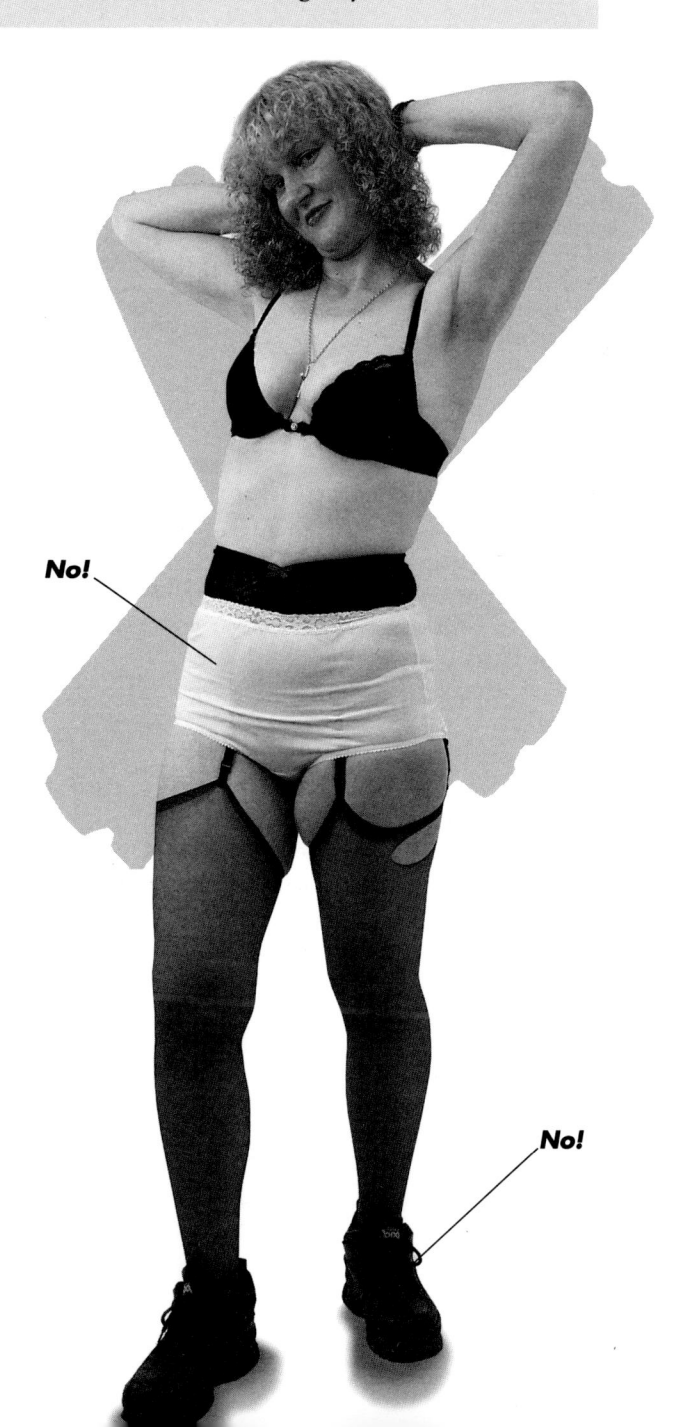

No!

No!

girl*power*

FACING UP TO THE "C"-WORD

Once upon a time a young man would get down on one knee and propose marriage to a young woman. The two of them would plight their troth in a place of worship, then they'd get a house, fill it with stuff and both live there with a selection of children until one of them died. Today, things aren't so simple.

In the 1960s, free love and feminism gave us some different models for relationships. Nowadays, we can be single, cohabit, get wed then get divorced, be celibate or bed hop and we won't be stoned in the street for bringing about The Downfall of Society.

Wonderfully liberating though all this is, we now have a new problem: commitment phobia. We've got so much choice about relationships, we're scared of saying we'll stick with one partner forever. Modern men are famously lousy at this, but modern women can be just as bad. So why are we gagging on the words, "You're my one and only"?

REASONS WHY WE WON'T COMMIT

MEN

- He's frightened of being smothered by a suffocating woman who might restrict his "masculine" activities, like watching the *101 Top Goals In History* video every night for three years.
- He's terrified of the female hysterical tantrum that could follow the break-up of a serious relationship (women being good at appallingly inventive acts of spite e.g. Mrs John Wayne Bobbit).
- He can father sprogs at any time of life so there's no biological pressure on him to settle down *en famille* (though what little kid wants a ninety-year-old deaf dribbling dad?)
- He likes the image of himself as a suave sexy stud-muffin. (Favoured line: "don't crowd me babe…")
- He worships women, seeing them as fascinating goddesses of crystalline perfection: so he won't want to live with one and find out she stuffs snotty tissues under the sofa cushions and cleans her toenails with the cutlery.

WOMEN

- She saw how her mother suffered (far too much housework and not enough fun).
- The pressure of being a modern woman means she sacrifices long-term love for a slow climb up the career ladder to Shoulder-Padded Executive Bitch Nirvana.
- She's so hopelessly insecure she thinks that any man who really wants her must be barking mad.
- She fancies herself as a fabulous *femme fatale*, and enjoys laughing merrily at the hordes of besotted suitors whom she picks up, uses and drops at her whim. (Favoured line: "Peel me a grape, boy…")
- She thinks all men are basically untrustworthy and wouldn't last five minutes "settled down" with a wife before being forced by male biological imperative to bonk their secretaries.

DON'T CROWD ME BABE…

MEN AND WOMEN

- We don't want responsibility: " I'll have to be grown-up... and live in suburbia... and get life insurance... and look after them when I can't even look after myself... It's too much like hard work... Aaaaaargh!"
- What if you said "Yes" to someone and the next week Tom Cruise split up with Nicole Kidman and he/she asked you out?
- It's a lot of fun being on your own.

HOW TO AVOID COMMITMENT WHILST STILL HAVING A PARTNER

Go out with
- Married men
- Gays (if you're straight)
- Straights (if you're gay)
- Lovers who live at least 100 miles away (preferably in New Zealand)
- Prisoners (preferably on Death Row)
- Soldiers
- Oil riggers
- Sir Ranulph Fiennes

HOW TO SPOT A PERSON WHO DOESN'T WANT TO COMMIT

- They've had three zillion previous relationships
- They keep forgetting your name
- They never leave their toothbrush
- They don't let you meet their parents
- Babies make them flinch
- You've been engaged to them for fifteen years

REASONS WHY IT'S GOOD TO COMMIT

- You get cuddled every night
- It's cheaper to buy a two-person house
- Your mum stops worrying about you
- When your brain's not working, you can let them think for you

PEEL ME A GRAPE, BOY...

IN THE END...

Seeing one partnership through thick and thin can be deeply satisfying, but it might be too much for you (a five-course dinner with all the trimmings). Bonking around a lot gives shorter, sweeter highs and subsequent lows (coffee and chocolate). Celibacy can be calm and untroubled, if a little boring (a big bowl of porridge). You choose what nourishes you.

Bon appetit!

girl*power*

confidential GIRLIE CHATS

A couple should never exist in a vacuum. It's vital that each partner sees other people, or the relationship will become too close and suffocating and paranoid. Of course, you don't think this is right at the beginning, when your eyes are glazed with love and cherubs follow in your footsteps. But the time will come when you need to talk to someone other than your lover; especially because you need to talk about him.

Enter your girlfriend, that trusty soul you've known for years who can always be relied upon to share a family-size tub of Double Chocolate Chip Toffee Ice-Cream With Extra Chocolate with you, as well as all your most intimate secrets. Of course the arrangement is reciprocal: if she needs to splurge her feelings about her latest beau, she need only say the word and you'll have the cushions plumped and a bottle of soave sweating in the ice-bucket. That's what friends are for.

SPILLING THE BEANS

With a good girlfriend you feel safe telling her everything including:

- A blow by blow account of what you do in the bedroom, sparing no squelchy details.
- The full biography, including family details and the relationship history of your man.
- Where you went on a date, including the plot of the movie, what you both ate in the restaurant and who paid for what.
- A full critique of his clothes, hair and facial features. ("I love the jagged cheek-bones, but those grey plastic shoes are going to have to go.")
- His unsavoury habits. ("He reheats leftover coffee, he scratches in bed, he collects dead insects.")
- His delightful habits. ("He tells me bedtime stories, he does all my handwashing, he laughs at all my jokes.")
- A blow by blow account of your rows. ("And then he said to me I was a stinky old cow and then I hit him with the blender…")
- What you think the future holds. ("If he shaves off the beard and gets promotion, I'll have his children; if not, I'm going to ask out that boy in accounts.")

and then he said…

…he didn't

*girl**power***

GETTING FEEDBACK
THE RESPONSE YOU NEED FROM HER

- Deeply sympathetic listening, with lots of nods, oohs and aahs, laughter where appropriate and "Oh you poor thing" when necessary.
- No judgement – you might be slagging him off, but if she says "I always thought he was a bit slimy" she's overstepping the mark: you love the guy for God's sake!
- Comparable stories from her experience that might illuminate your situation ("I too went out with a man who collected dead insects…").
- No changing the subject: when you're having a good wallow, you don't want her saying: "Anyway, did I tell you about the great saving I made on four packs of oven-chips at Safeways?"
- No motherly advice, like "Pull yourself together", "Boys will be boys", "He'd love you more if you dyed your hair and wore a bit of lipstick".

WHAT'S SHE GETTING OUT OF IT?

- It's riveting stuff: there's nothing more entertaining than tales about the nitty-gritty of love.
- It's educational: she can learn some good tips about how to carry on in her own relationships.
- She can feel a lot better about her own problems if you're in a bit of a love-pickle.
- A need for the sick-bucket when you're on a sentimental rant about what a darling honey-bunny sweetie-pants he is.
- A smug feeling of self-worth that you chose her to confide in.

WHAT ARE YOU GETTING OUT OF IT?

- A sense of perspective: spilling the beans helps you to take a clear look at all those confusing thoughts and feelings that have been churning around inside you.
- A way forward in the relationship: maybe the guy is an out-and-out loser, but it took telling your friend to realize it, or maybe you were down on him, but telling her his good points lets you see he is a pretty good bloke.
- Total attention from someone who loves and respects you and thinks you're a wonderful human being (which, let's face it, you're not always gonna get from that big lump you're dating…).

girl*power*

the rules on BREAKING UP

When you have really loved someone, there is no such thing as a painless break-up. Even when you're happily whooping "Yippee! I've ditched the bastard!" a little gremlin of sadness can pop up and cause a shudder of ruefulness or a spasm of grief. At its worst, splitting up causes eternal misery and shattered lives. But that needn't be your story if you follow these tips.

IF HE DUMPED YOU:

You must release your anger and deal with the loss of pride. REVENGE may help.
For instance you could:

- Destroy his property, especially any state-of-the-art computers, hi-fis or cards, rare record and tape collections, football memorabilia or any piece of DIY handiwork that took him months to craft to perfection. Be careful: a friend of ours set fire to her ex's Trivial Pursuit game – stupidly she did it on her own carpet and burnt it through to the floorboards. We think this was a sign that she should've picked something a lot more meaningful.
- Fill in innumerable junk-mail applications with his name and address.
- When he's on holiday get into his flat, dial the speaking clock and leave the receiver off, for however many days or weeks he's away…

However if you want to avoid criminal proceedings, try these:

- Make an effigy in his image from candle wax and give it a good stab every time you feel miserable about him.
- Use photographs of him instead of litter in the cat tray.
- Play squash – every thwack of the ball against the wall can be a metaphorical smack in his face.
- That's enough anger; now you need to put yourself back together again. So…
- Go on holiday, somewhere you've never been – this will help to remind you of how well you can function without him and won't set off too many memory-triggers.
- Make a radical change to your appearance (preferably something he would have hated) e.g. get a nose-ring, crop your hair or buy purple coloured contact lenses.
- Move house, you won't want to stay anywhere he's been.

IF YOU DUMPED HIM

You will have an initial burst of euphoria and feel very powerful and in control. Use this energy to take your life by the short and curlies and give it a good shake. What parts of your life could be functioning better? Work? Home? Health? Attack them with all the vigour of a woman who's just got rid of one thing that wasn't working for her and is keen to scythe down some more.

Your momentum will slow down after a while. You may feel guilt, loss, nostalgia or a smidgen of loneliness. But have faith in your decision to quit. If it felt right when you said "Dave you're a schmuck and I'm taking the car," it's still right now.

Make a list of all the advantages of being apart from him.
1. No more dog-ends in the pot-plants
2. Freedom

There's two for starters.

WHOEVER DUMPS WHO

When you need to cry, do it: it's better out than in. But if real depression threatens (symptoms: forgetting to eat, physical immobility, watching Open University programmes about open-cast zinc mining), get some friends around you quickly. You'll be amazed how much of your misery they'll be willing to put up with and they can feed you and remind you which shoe goes on which foot and how to use a hairbrush.

Avoid the temptation to ring him up a lot. You're bound to have unfinished business with him, but the two of you are the wrong people to be each others' therapists. Whatever you do, don't hold out big hopes for getting back together – this break was a crisis that needed to happen, so use it to have a good look at your own life and what you want from it.

One sure-fire way of getting over an old lover is to pick up a new one (and a fresh, affectionate and obliging male is not to be sniffed at). But if you're a serial monogamist (that is, you have boyfriends or husbands back to back, so to speak) you should try solo for a while. Don't get off with any old bloke just to plaster over the wounds from your ex. There's no need to be grateful for some crummy hairy slimeball geezer just because your ego's been knocked for six and you need a cuddle.

And finally… if he does come grovelling back to you, promising he'll change if you can get together again, be kind, don't laugh too hard as you send him on his way. (But the delicious sight of a grown man begging will give you many hours of amusement in retrospect…)

HOW TO MAKE THE FIRST MOVE

We British are so uptight about making the first move – it's a miracle there are ever any babies born. Think of a typical chat-up scenario and it usually involves a beery bloke slurring something obscene. But girls don't have to be like that. What you need is assertiveness, determination and a little wit, and be ready to say *"C'est la vie"* if he turns you down. What the hell – embarrassment only lasts a few minutes, but if you don't at least try, you could be passing up the love of your life. What you need is an opener, any opener.

AT A PARTY

- Tell him you're doing research on a book about love and would he give you his views on the best chat-up lines?
- Say you're learning palm-reading and could you practise on him?
- Drop your earring in his vicinity and ask him to help you find it.
- Say "I'm sick of asking strangers the same old 'What do you do?' line, so I'm going to try something different: 'how would you decorate your ideal bathroom?' Or 'What are your top ten songs of all time?' or 'If you had to spend all your money in one shop, which one would it be?'"
- Accidentally on purpose spill drink on his thigh (then whip out some tissues and pat it dry).

AT A CLUB

- Ask him if he is a professional dancer (of course he's not, but hey, any guy who's brave enough to get up and dance deserves the out-and-out lie when it comes to flattery).
- Ask the DJ to play a record for him (try to make it appropriate: "You're the First, My Last, My Everything", however, might be just a little bit strong for a first move though...).
- Tell him you're keen to revive old dance styles and would he be kind enough do the foxtrot with you?

ON THE TRAIN

- To a nice man reading a newspaper – ask him to read your stars.
- Get him to help you with that ever so tricky crossword clue.
- Ask him where he bought those fabulous boots/trousers/ear-muffs.

IN A CAFÉ
- Ask him if he'd recommend a sandwich.
- Spread out some travel brochures, agonize over them, then turn to him and say, "What do you think, Balearics, Bombay or Blackpool?"
- Tell him he has *cappuccino* froth on his upper lip (sweetly of course).

IN THE PUB
- Buy him a drink.
- Ask him to play pool or darts or team up with you in the pub quiz.
- Tell him your friend's stood you up and could you borrow his mobile phone to see where she is? Pretend she said she's ill and not coming and oh dear, now you're at a loose end…

IN THE STREET
- Take a camera everywhere and ask any likely chaps if they'd mind posing for a new photo-series you're doing called "Trendy Men About Town".
- Take a tape recorder and microphone everywhere and do research for a new radio programme on "How to talk to strangers".
- Tell him you've lost your dog, and "here's my phone number in case you spot Spot".

IN THE LIBRARY
- Check out the book he's picked out and say "Oh dear, that's the one I wanted" (WARNING: you might be in trouble if it's *Advanced Particle Physics*).

ON A TRAIN PLATFORM
- Pretend you've got an irritating speck of dirt in your eye. Well, it worked for Celia Johnson in *Brief Encounter*…

IF YOU KNOW HIM ALREADY:
- Invite him to a party at your house ("cos I'm short of lovely men").
- Ask him round to fix your car/computer/shelves/video/love-life.
- Ring him up and ask him out (we know it's obvious, but why pussyfoot around?).

AT THE SWIMMING BATHS
- Ask him to give you tips on your breaststroke.

IF YOU JUST CAN'T SPEAK FIRST:
Wear a very tight red dress, a Wonderbra and an enigmatic smile and stand under a light. He'll come to you.

A GUIDE TO HOLIDAY *ROMANCE*

The huge mistake that girls make when they take up with a gorgeous specimen a long way from home is taking the affair much too seriously. Charged up by cheap plonk and the giddy romance of balmy nights on the sea-shore, we often start believing "This guy is it!" It's best to ban this idea from your mind before you even start fluttering your eyelashes at the waiters. Go into your far-flung fling with the attitude that you want some fun, a bit of company, an ego-boost or an adventure. That way you won't waste a few hundred quid mooning about over some Lanzarote Lothario, when you should be having a nice relaxing break. With that in mind, here are some of the situations that you should prepare yourselves for when holidays and romance meet.

YOU GET A CRUSH ON SOMEONE

You see him at breakfast, in the bar or collecting deckchairs; he's got a lovely smile, a washboard stomach and he doesn't appear to be taken. Whenever you get within ten feet of him, your heart jumps and you can't stop giggling like a schoolgirl. Your friends get a lot of mileage out of teasing you about him. This goes on for two weeks, until the last night when you finally get to snog him and discover his breath smells like old cabbage.

YOU GO FOR A BLOKE WHO JUST ISN'T YOUR TYPE

It's slim-pickings time at your chosen resort/youth hostel/barge trip down the Congo. All the tasty types are already coupled and all that's left for you is a skinny guy with fair hair and a morbid interest in fish. (When you usually go for big guys with dark hair and a morbid interest in mammals.) What the hell, you'll have "Skinny" anyway.

YOU DON'T SPEAK EACH OTHER'S LANGUAGE

The relationship is conducted entirely through smiles, gestures, winks, petting, snogging and full-throttle sexual shenanigans. If only you had bothered to swot up a few key phrases from the guidebook on the plane… still, like Eric Cantona, he sounds indecipherable but dead exotic. Just make sure you're not nodding cheerfully to a question that you think means "Do you fancy an ice-cream?" but actually means "Will you give up your life to live with me in a hovel, wear a veil, milk goats and bear me endless children?".

YOU FALL FOR THE TOUR GUIDE

Every other female, from sixteen to sixty, has done the same; there's nothing like a well-informed young man taking charge to set girls' hearts a-racing. You follow him around like a lost puppy and cook up questions for him that will make you sound fascinating (less "Where are the toilets?" more "I hear there are some Minoan temple ruins in the forest…"). When you get him into the forest, you either find out he's a sporty anorak with no sense of humour, or that he's an incorrigible shagger who can't resist exploiting his hero status.

YOU GO AWAY WITH A PLATONIC MALE FRIEND

Within three days, he's leapt on you. You give him a good smack and tell him not to be ridiculous. After a week without so much as a flirt elsewhere you leap on him.

YOU MAKE IT WITH AN IMPOVERISHED LOCAL

You've spotted a beautiful man and the fact he's a fisherman/road sweeper/rickshaw carrier is entirely irrelevant. You love his simplicity, his closeness to nature, his rough strong hands. He loves the fact that if he can get you to marry him, he can get the hell out of his terrible job and come and live in a wealthy country with better prospects. Don't give him your phone number.

YOU'VE PAIRED OFF WITH THE FRIEND OF THE BLOKE WHO'S AFTER YOUR MATE

AND he's always a geek. You don't want to go off in a sulk on your own, so you stick around with the foursome, fighting off "Geek-Man" every time he offers to rub lotion on your back. At best, you discover a grudging gratitude for him, as at least there's someone to take the mickey out of when you're bored watching your mate and her beau tongue-wrestling.

YOU BONK EVERYTHING IN (HAWAIIAN) SHORTS

You meet Tom on Monday but he's leaving the next day so you move on to Tony, who's nice but a bit fat. So you shift to Trevor, use him up in two days and then go on to Terry the porter at the hotel. By the time you've got to Tim – the pilot of the plane on the way home, you seriously need a holiday.

YOU BARGE OFF WITH A BACK-PACKER

He talks to you in a café and seduces you with tales of Nepal, Kashmir and Cambodia. You see yourself riding camels at sunset, climbing majestic mountains, sleeping on remote beaches and skinny-dipping at dawn. You end up begging in Bangkok, with nothing to your name but a woolly pixie-hat, a festering sleeping-bag and a battered diary of seventeen months on the road. When you get home, you never see him again.

HOWEVER, IT HAS BEEN KNOWN…

You meet a lovely, bright, attractive, well-adjusted man and have a perfect time swimming, eating and making passionate love. You marry him and live ecstatically ever after.
ONCE IN A BLUE MOON!

*girl*power

HOW TO KEEP AN INTEREST IN YOUR LOVER'S CAREER

Whether he's an artist, chef or accountant, his career can become your dullest topic of conversation. When he tells you about his day do you:
a) listen intently, taking it all in?
b) look interested, nodding in all the right places?
c) fall into a coma?
d) move to another country?

If your answer to this question is something other than a) then it's time to remember that you love (nearly) everything about him, especially the way that he finds your own career entirely fascinating. Therefore it's time to return the favour and to start taking an interest in his career.

THE TOP FIVE BORING CAREERS TO ATTEMPT AN INTEREST IN

ACCOUNTANT
ZZZZzzzz . . . oops sorry. This is probably not the best response. However, finding numbers and tax returns at all stimulating is going to be a difficult task. Dumping him is the obvious option, but if you really love him become self-employed, and then you will need an accountant. Receiving the free service should result in an immediate interest in his returns.

CIVIL ENGINEER
This sounds a bit like a bloke that fixes your car but in a civilized way. Whatever the job entails, the word engineer conjures up the word DULL. However, as with accountants, if you really must be with this man then the best thing you can do is first find out exactly what he does. This is sufficient interest in this type of job.

ESTATE AGENT
He's the total scum of the earth but you still want to keep him, so show your interest by speaking to him in his own language. Tell him that his "roof doesn't need much maintenance" and his "back garden, although north facing" – i.e. sees little sun – "has a country feel to it" – i.e. it stinks – and that he's a "bargain at the price" – i.e. he's cheap. In short, dump him or get him to buy you a house.

4. COMPUTER PROGRAMMER
If he's got sufficient RAM he's worth hanging on to. Invest in a few computer games and if you can play network "Command and Conquer" with him, you'll have a mate for life.

5. LIBRARIAN
Listen intently to his tales of the microfiche and if he starts to bore you say "Shhhhhhhhhh".

If he happens to have a glamorous job this can seem very exciting at first. But it won't be long before the novelty wears off and he might as well be talking stocks and shares rather than his opening night at the National Theatre.

THE TOP FIVE MOST INTERESTING JOBS

1. PERFORMER
This breed requires more interest than any other profession. Whether he's an actor, comedian or musician he'll demand your full attention and will accuse you of ruining his career if he doesn't get it. They require very patient partners so it helps if you're a groupie, star shagger or have no life of your own. For us mere mortals, the best thing to do, when he's telling you for the seventh time how he stormed the gig, is to listen patiently aided by a bottle of Jack Daniels, several spliffs and Prozac.

2. MASSEUR
Probably the most fantastic career a woman could hope for in a bloke. By nature the masseur is a patient, attentive man – what sort of person gives that many massages without getting one in return? This is the one time you want his work life to spill over into his personal life and you might as well make the most of it. Find the baby oil, lie back and willingly listen to his arduous day.

3. DETECTIVE
Don't ever be fooled into thinking that you'll end up with Bodie or Doyle. You're more likely to end up with Miss Marple. The one big plus about this job is that they are rarely allowed to talk about their work, to which you reply: "That's okay darling, I understand." The drawback though, is that you could never go looking for a sneaky love-affair behind his back and remain uncaught, after all it is part of their job to catch cheats.

4. GRAPHIC DESIGNER
Learn phrases such as "wow, just look at the juxtaposition between the curves and perspective" and insert them into any sentence, giving the impression that you understand depth and space and other such boring bollocks that graphic designers crap on about.

5. DOCTOR
Keep up to date with *Casualty*, *ER* and *The Young Doctors*. This should give you all the information you need to appear knowledgeable to your own young doctor. However, never try to diagnose or interpret what he tells you, as it is a well-known fact that the doctor is always right. Yeah right!

Whatever the job, learn to sleep with your eyes open, nod in the right places and say "mm, I see" occasionally. If you can pull this off, FANTASTIC.

girl*power*

Valentine's Cards

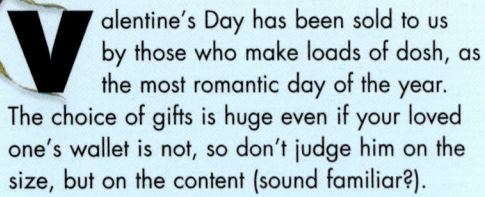

Valentine's Day has been sold to us by those who make loads of dosh, as the most romantic day of the year. The choice of gifts is huge even if your loved one's wallet is not, so don't judge him on the size, but on the content (sound familiar?).

There is just one article that every teenage girl dreams of finding in her letterbox on the 14th of February and that something is singular and long with a red end. Three, four or even a dozen is great, but the production of one solitary red rose is enough to make even the most hardened virgin succumb to her over-hormonal boyfriend. If you don't have the good fortune to find that your man is sensitive to your material needs (or is indeed desperate and cleverly manipulative) then here are some other gifts for first time lovers.

FLUFFY TOY
With or without "I luv U" emblazoned on a fluffy heart, depending on whether or not you come from Essex.

ANY OTHER FLOWERS
Except lilies which are for funerals (or could he be trying to tell you something?).

PERFUME
Except if it's anything he purchased from a man with a suitcase in the local high street, when it's time to dump him for bad taste.

CHOCOLATES
Hopefully your loved one will be selective and you'll be receiving a hand wrapped box of Belgian truffles, but hey, chocolates are chocolates.

girl*power*

Those of us who have turned down the "Tramp" and chucked because of "Charlie" have probably, at one time or another, entered into what is known as the "long-term relationship". Here, you've been through the flowers, the fluffy toys and even the forgotten Valentine's Days and it's time for him to be inventive. You should, by now, have enough Chanel No 5 to scent a small country, so here are some tips for long-term lovers, Valentine's gifts.

VIBRATOR
Receive this with the good humour hopefully intended or it could make for an ugly day.

UNDERWEAR
Accept this gift lovingly as it takes a lot of guts (and beers) for a man to seriously walk into Knickerbox and ask the assistant to recommend something for his beloved whilst trying to avoid an erection. If he does turn up with crotchless knickers and peek-a-boo bras, then he's either seriously kinky or desperately naive. Either way try to be grateful for the effort shown.

BODY SHOP FOOT WASH
You've obviously been together far too long or he's just revealed his true colours as an insensitive plonker.
Either way it's time for your love life to move on.

With love X

OTHER STRANGE VALENTINE'S CARDS OF THE FUTURE

"Got a card from your wife, your boring bride? Well here's a big one from your bit on the side."
(Mistress)

"I know we're related, but I like you the best, What's really wrong with a bit of incest?"
(Small villages in Devon or *Brookside*)

"Your hair is so curly, I think you're a star It makes me so horny when you go baaa."
(Wales)

THE HIGHS AND LOWS OF ROMANCE WITH THE Older Man

Defining "the older man" depends on your own age at the time. At the age of eight, a boy of eight and a half seems like your grandad, whereas at forty, a bloke of fifty is a spring chicken. It will always be super cool for any teenager to go out with an older guy, the nearer to your dad's age (if you're Mandy Smith) the cooler.

Girls associate age with wisdom. This is a BIG MISTAKE. The only thing men acquire with age is more bullshit and less hair.

WHY AN OLDER GUY WANTS A YOUNGER GIRL

1 Because women of their own age think that they're a jerk and wouldn't put up with "listen to all my interesting travels on the road stories".
2 'Cos he wants firm breasts attached to a giggling machine.
3 He's a paedophile.
4 Because he's a man.

WHY A YOUNGER GIRL WANTS AN OLDER GUY

1 'Cos she wants to lose her virginity to a more experienced lover.
2 Boys of her own age are "so immature".
3 'Cos she likes flabby stomachs, thinning hair and dentures.
4 'Cos he's a really good cook.
5 Because she's a regular at Stringfellows and that's all she can find there.
6 Because she has severe psychological problems.

DISASTROUS OLDER-GUY RELATIONSHIPS OF OUR TIME

PRINCE CHARLES AND LADY DI
It wasn't the age difference that was so much a problem here. It was the classic case of "he may be ugly but he's a prince" that happens to us all the time. The fact that Charles actually preferred to find true love with a woman who looks more like his mum also had something to do with the inevitable break-up.

MANDY SMITH AND BILL WYMAN

Bill could hardly wait until Mand was out of nappies before he started dating her. Mind you, after all those years of drugs, goo goo ga ga was probably the full extent of Bill's vocab. Again the whole thing ended in disaster when Mandy finally woke up one morning from what she thought was a bad dream. Sadly it was real life – she'd hit puberty and thought she was in bed with her grandad.

SINGERS WHO MARRY THEIR RECORD COMPANY OWNERS
(MARIAH CAREY)

With all that time spent singing those high notes they must have just forgotten to ask for young virile lovers on their Christmas stocking list. What they've ended up with is a wrinkly with a very large wallet and a never-ending record contract. Clever.

WHERE LOVE WITH THE OLDER MAN BREAKS DOWN

Not to sound too cynical, but they inevitably do break down sooner rather than later, if not through divorce then through a heart bypass operation. Even though the initial stages of this type of relationship can be fun, eventually the cracks of era difference will start to show. Here are a few common ones:

1 When he goes on about the first Seekers' concert he went to and you've never heard of them.
2 He buys you a recipe book for Spicy Grills when you had asked for Spice Girls.
3 He starts to get on better with your parents than with you.
4 When you say you want a house party he goes to the local freezer centre to buy the vol-au-vents.
5 When you tell him you've taken an "E" he thinks it's time to buy a new Scrabble set.

Don't worry, it's not all doom and gloom. There are some positive things:

1 He may be a genuinely nice bloke who just happens to like you for what you are and not for the pertness of your breasts.
2 If he's got lots of dosh and he's a lot older, he's more likely to die before you, leaving you a very desirable rich widow (make sure you check out his insurance policies first).
3 He'll buy you lots of presents to keep you. Hooray.

*girl*power

INTRODUCING HIM TO MUM AND DAD

At what point is it the right time to introduce your loved one to mum and dad? For some people it's on the second date and for others it's not until the birth of your fifth child. Try to assess the S & C (Scare and Commitment) factor of your beau. Obviously you're on to a winner when he utters the words "When can I meet your folks?". However, the chances of this happening are about the same as getting him to do the ironing. So, vast amounts of tact and cunning are needed when approaching this subject (and if you can get him to think that it was his idea all along then you're laughing).

But it's fate and not love that plays a major part in getting him to meet mum and dad. The sun is shining down on you if a member of your family just happens to be having a huge wedding with loads of free grub and booze, after all what man can resist complimentary catering and cans of Special Brew? However, if you're a mere mortal with Sod's law on your side you're going to have to raise the issue very carefully. Here are some of the settings in which you can introduce him to your parents.

1 Invite your parents round without telling your loved one. A bit sneaky? Of course! But if your parents can be just a bit discreet and not say things like "We've been dragged round here so we can take a look at a future member of our family" then things should run pretty smoothly.

2 Invite the olds round for dinner and suggest that you both cook dinner (see "Real Together Things to Do"). This has a slight disadvantage not present in no.1. He has time to get nervous, worked up and possibly do a runner before the horsd'oeuvres. Take him to your parents' house for drinks/dinner/Trivial Pursuit. If, when you suggest this, he says that maybe you've been seeing too much of each other and it's time to slow things down a bit, reassure him that if he wants to leave early then you are prepared (because you love him and think he's the best boyfriend short of Brad Pitt) to fake any disease that he likes and you can both politely dash off.

3

THE MEETING

The success of the first meeting vastly depends on the religion of your family. Atheist is generally all right whereas Muslim parents can mean him making a sharp exit. Read on to learn more ...

JEWISH

If your man isn't a doctor or lawyer or some other fantastically upwardly mobile professional then prepare your mother in advance (or risk a coronary). Tell her that it doesn't matter that he's only been to the polytechnic of life and spent a bit of time at Her Majesty's Pleasure, he's the man you love and cherish and he's prepared to be circumcised if that's what it takes. Eventually daddy will realize that if this is the man his little baby loves then that is what they will put up with, and welcome him with open arms (but closed wallets).

CATHOLIC

One thing your boyfriend must not say when meeting Catholic parents is: "Your daughter's great in bed and we're moving in together." The first part is not as bad as the second, because the mere thought of their precious daughter living in sin is something they may never get over. Another no-no is: "It's all right we're using condoms."

AGNOSTIC

These parents are usually very liberal and will be gagging to meet any boyfriend of any kind, the more unusual the better. However you must prepare him for the inevitable "twenty questions". They will want to know every intimate detail of his, his parents', his cats' and your sex lives. This is not because they are nosy, it's just that they want to appear interested and open-minded in everything that their offspring chooses to do.

CHURCH OF ENGLAND
AND OTHER FÊTE-THROWING RELIGIONS

This is probably the easiest of situations in which to introduce blokes to the folks. Anything goes really. If he happens to mention that you go like a rabbit, it will most likely go unnoticed so long as he's scoffing on your mum's scones at the time, saying: "Wow! These are the best scones ever. You must win prizes with these. Can I have some more?"

THE RULES ON MOVING IN TOGETHER

Moving in together is something that can happen at any time, from your second date to a month after you're married (or never in the case of Woody and Mia). Obviously the most appropriate time is somewhere in between the time you find out his embarrassing middle name and being invited to his family Christmas dinner. Make sure that the decision to move in together is a mutual one. It won't work if you suddenly turn up on his doorstep with all your worldly belongings saying you've come to rearrange his flat and that you might as well stay there permanently after it's done. Likewise, you don't want him gradually moving his things in without your noticing, until one day you realize that his motorbike-mag subscription starts arriving at your address and he invites his friends round to "our" house.

Moving in together involves the "c" word –
COMMITMENT.
For her It means that you can't strop off to your own home after a tiff.
For him It means no more private sessions watching *Baywatch* with a box of tissues.
Here are some pros and cons of living together.

PROS

SEX ON TAP
This may sound great in theory, but it very rarely lives up to the hype. After all, when you're only allowed to have your favourite pudding twice a week it tastes absolutely yummy, but when you're allowed to have it every night of the week, and more at weekends, you may start to feel a bit sick.

PERMANENT BACK SCRUBBER
Having baths together without the chance of a flatmate walking in is fab, but beware, unless you have a huge bath, you'll end up with the "tap end" argument.

PERSONAL TELEPHONE ANSWERING SERVICE
Only a good thing if you surgically implant a pad and pen to his body, as the chances are you'll end up with the equivalent of a Betacom Answerphone that records the messages from your mum but decides to erase the one about the big night out.

INHERITING EQUIPMENT
If you've never owned a computer, CD player or Scalextric set, the chances are you'll probably end up with one or more of these items. When moving in together, all items suddenly have dual ownership. However, make sure he understands the rules: this does not apply to anything belonging to you of course. Do be sure to explain this to him very carefully.

CONS

TOILET SEAT PROBLEMS

1 To be up or to be down – that is the argument. This could be settled by whose house you move into. If he moves in with you then it stays down and vice versa, but you're more likely to find a new place together. This problem has been at the centre of some very messy divorce settlements so try and sort it out quickly and quietly (i.e. down).

PERSONAL BATHROOM SMELLS

2 Fact: boys are smellier than girls! Enough said!

COOKING

3 Unless you're lucky enough to have moved in with the entire team of *Ready Steady Cook*, then you are probably going to end up doing the majority of the meal making. At first this seems quite romantic, preparing delicious delicacies for the man you love. But after a few months of watching him inhale the lovingly prepared cuisine without so much as an "mmmmm", the desire quickly wears off. You can try telling him that it's his turn to whip up something for you – if you really want to eat a dodgy meat pie with alphabet fries. The best you can hope for is demanding to be taken out for a meal every so often, making sure that it burns a substantial hole in his pocket.

> Moving in together is what you make it. For some of us it is the excuse to turn into your mum. Not a good idea. RESIST. Whoever said "Love means never having to say you're sorry" was talking out of their arse. Even if you don't mean it, say it. Make life easy and have a laugh.

girl*power*

ADVICE FOR YOUR WEDDING NIGHT

One of the greatest pressures of your wedding day is not the "I do's" or even your father's embarrassing speech. It's the unmentioned "must" that occurs after the last piece of cake has been devoured by the dog and the final dregs of champagne have been swallowed by your pissed-up Uncle Gerald. The thing we're talking about is the wedding night LOVE-MAKING.

Before the night arrives you may be thinking "I have to have sex? Fantastic!"

Imagine, after you've eaten enough food to feed a small northern town and drunk enough booze to make the food you've eaten be available again, then the last thing you will feel like is finding your way out of your whalebone wedding dress, putting your cap in and looking pretty all at the same time.

Here are a few tips to put you in the mood for love on your wedding night.

1 Just because there is tons of yummy food available and your parents keep reminding you of all the money they have spent on it, this doesn't mean you have to have every last prawn vol-au-vent (even though they are your favourites and you requested them specially). Limit yourself and never get too full, after all, your husband-to-be doesn't want you chucking when he gives you a passionate snog on the dance floor (and it doesn't look too good in the wedding video either).

2 Alcohol is probably the single most important issue in the "fun on the Kingsize" front. It is a very difficult one to get right. Too little, and you have the urge to continue talking to Auntie Mary about her verruca. Too much, and you have the urge to talk to the toilet bowl. If you get it right then you're on for a fun night of passion and frolics.

3 Getting married is a knackering thing. Getting dolled up, getting nervous, getting bored by relatives and getting very sore feet. This means that getting laid is not at the top of your list of priorities when all you feel like doing is getting some sleep.

Pace yourself. Spend the previous two weeks sleeping or, if all else fails, take enough Pro Plus to keep you awake till your ninetieth birthday. Spend as much of the day as possible sitting down. (If you can have a chair at the altar then great – especially useful at Catholic weddings.)

Another potential (if not certain) problem is the issue of the drunken husband. There's no point in taking care of yourself if, when you get to the boudoir you find yourself lying beside a snoring, farting wreck that has as much chance of an erection as the Millennium Tower.

You could try appealing to his "new man" side and ask him nicely, not to drink for England on your big day. If this appears not to sink in, then there's only one thing for it. Be sneaky. Try anything. Water down his drinks, lie, cheat, anything as long as he can still stand without an aid and can hold a coherent conversation on something other than football.

THE BEDROOM

This could be anywhere from the first night in your brand new house (in your dreams), to a hotel room in Blackpool, to your own grotty bedsit. Wherever it is, make it special. Prepare a small hamper of bagels and orange juice for stamina, aromatic-oil burners for sensuality and porn films for a laugh. Here are some more things you can try to get you both in the mood for lurrve.

1 Have a bath together with just candles for light. The only danger here is that you may fall asleep only to wake up the next morning feeling cold and wet.

2 Wear the sexiest underwear you can find. This doesn't necessarily mean crotchless knickers and peek-a-boo bras, but if that's what he's into then go for it just this once, after all it's his night too.

3 If all else fails have some black cherry yoghurt/peanut butter/chocolate spread on hand. Or, if you're not feeling peckish you can use the bagels (as mentioned earlier) to play hoopla on his knob.

The most important thing is to have fun, and if you really don't feel up to a night of lovemaking you are allowed to save it for the morning, just never tell anyone 'cos he'll never live it down.

Romantic Music to get you in the Mood

This all depends on what mood you want to be put in. Most likely, you'll want to be in the mood for "lurve", but you might want to get in the mood for low-down dirty raw sex.

"Lurve" can cover a whole spectrum from an evening in holding hands to that dirty, raw sex thing.

We'll start with the tame and work our way up to the wicked.

ANYTHING BY SADE

1 She's always a safe bet for first dates or young love. You'll never have to edit any of her albums, as none of the songs speed up to anything above smooch pace. If you don't want the hassle of changing the CD, just set it to continuous play and the chances are neither of you will notice the CD repeating. This is not because you are so engrossed in one another but because all Sade songs sound the same.

BARRY WHITE

2 This is for the more serious smoochers. It may seem corny but it'll get the most uptight of you in the mood for some "tongue tango-ing". We're sure there are some subliminal messages going on under the music, as many couples have even claimed to have conceived to Barry (his music, not him personally!).

PRINCE

3 Be very careful – only listen to his old stuff to get you in the mood for a night of wild love. Listening to the newer crap ("Bet You By Golly Wow" – enough said) is more likely to make you go than come. Especially good is the *Purple Rain* album containing the very long version of the single "Purple Rain". Length of album is nearly as important as length of "the other". You don't want to be approaching heaven only to have to get off at the pearly gates to change the music, therefore sending you back to your bedroom.

OUR SONG

4 Everyone has an "our song", whether it's something they adore or loathe. There will always be a song that sticks and reminds you of those first few weeks of passionate fumbling. How many times have you heard the DJ at a wedding suddenly announce that the dance floor must be cleared so that the lovely couple can smooch to "their song"? If the song is anything by Lionel Richie then it's time for anyone with any taste to make a sharp exit before they chunder.

COOL "OUR SONGS"

1 Anything by the Spice Girls. Let him know who's boss.
2 "Femme Fatale" by The Velvet Underground. Too cool for words. Check it out!
3 "Fernando". Anything by ABBA is cool. Those of you who don't agree had better check out the uncool list for your song.
4 "Fever" by Peggy Lee (not Madonna). Phew.
5 "Let there be Love" by Nat King Cole. Still cool even though it does advertise pork.

DEFINITELY UNCOOL "OUR SONGS"

1 "Lady In Red" by Chris de Burgh. Especially uncool if red is his favourite colour.
2 "Hello" by Lionel Richie. Goodbye.
3 "Kayleigh" by Marillion. True story. It's time he got over it.
4 Anything by Peter André, Take That, Boyzone, The Backstreet Boys, Boys anything else.

RAVEL'S "BOLERO"

A piece of top French impressionist composing. The underlying theme keeps a steady, but seductive rhythm firmly in its grasp with the haunting melody juxtaposing the ostinato beautifully.

Unfortunately, this stunning piece of workmanship is completely and utterly ruined by the subconscious image of Dudley Moore trying to shag Bo Derek and not being able to get it up.

If you do, however, find yourself in the unfortunate position of attempted seduction to this music then you must run, don't walk, out of his flat to the nearest building site to find someone with a bit more sophistication.

MUSIC NOT TO HAVE ON YOUR SMOOCH COMPILATION TAPE
(unless you want to be chucked)

1 "Firestarter" by The Prodigy
2 The theme tune to The Simpsons
3 Military Marches (unless you're a bit kinky that way)
4 "I Should Be So Lucky" by Kylie Minogue
5 "The Frog Chorus" by Paul McCartney

Finally, here are some silly songs to have fun to. For use only in long-term relationships or he'll think you escaped from the local loony bin.

1 "Satisfaction" by The Rolling Stones (is this a hint?)
2 The theme tune to The Wombles
3 *Mission Impossible* theme
4 Housewives' Choice
5 "There's No-one Quite Like Grandma" by St Winifred's School Choir

girlpower

REAL TOGETHER THINGS TO DO

When you eventually decide that you want to do more things together, NEVER NEVER say "let's do something together". This sentence can strike fear into even the newest of men. They don't hear "let's do something together", they hear "let's spend the entire weekend at Ikea". Some of you are now thinking "not a bad idea", but you'll score no brownie points in suggesting this and will only confirm in his mind of your idea of "doing things together". It's always a good thing to try to turn it around so that he thinks that the whole experience was his idea. This can be done by slipping the Ideal Home Exhibition brochure into his lunch box (the sandwich variety) or putting the Ikea catalogue in with his secret supply of girlie mags (if you really insist on spending any time in that kiddy-ridden hell hole). BUT, the best way to keep love alive and enjoy "doing things together" is to find things that you might actually enjoy doing together. Failing that, suggest things that he wants to do and then call in that Ikea favour at a later date.

THINGS THAT HE LIKES TO DO

The Motor Show
This may seem like a bit of a drag, but get clued up on cars and it can be fun (especially when you're out with his mates and you can say things like "what an extremely powerful flux capacitor..." with complete confidence and watch their jaws drop). If you do decide to go to a vehicle related event AND genuinely enjoy it, he will think that you're the coolest girlfriend this side of Uma Thurman.

Sega World
Yes you're probably right in thinking "all joysticks and no loo paper", but computer games can be a lot of testosterone playing with even more software so put on your baseball cap, grab your bollocks and off you go to shoot a load of baddies. It's surprising how killing a load of blokes can lower your stress levels.

The Footie
You have just two choices in how to play this one. You can either join the boys and become all macho OR you can really hack them off by saying things like "which side is the bloke in the black shirt on" (followed by lots of giggling). This ensures that you will never ever be taken to a match again.

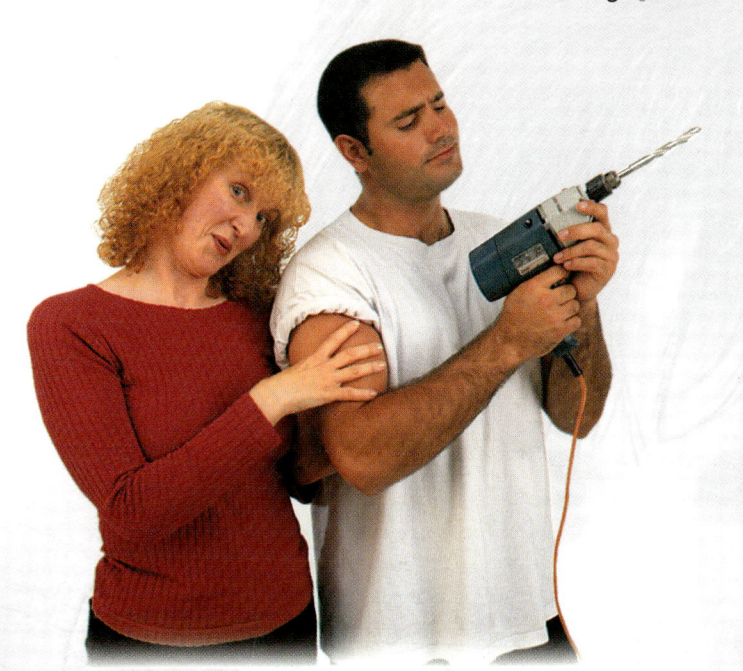

THINGS THAT YOU LIKE TO DO THAT YOU HAVE THE SLIGHTEST CHANCE OF HIM AGREEING TO

The Cinema

This sounds like an easy one but it obviously depends on the type of film you've got your heart set on (and whether they do a good selection of confectionery or not). Remember you waited a long time to see *Sense and Sensibility* and *Waiting To Exhale*. The only time a man is willing to see a girlie film is if you've been denying him his bloke rights and he thinks that seeing a girlie lovey film will suddenly cause you to be gagging for it. Let him think this, if it means getting your own way (but you could have a teensy problem if you don't follow through).

Cooking a Meal

You may now be thinking "as if!" – but wait. Suggest you make starters and main together and he can have strawberries and you for dessert. The whole thing is much more appealing if the entire meal is for you two only, so get dressed for dinner (promising him that you'll wear no knickers). The actual preparation can be loads of fun, especially if you do a "Keith Floyd" i.e. loads of booze. Even if you only end up with beans on toast with a side dish of tuna, eat it by candlelight and, if you're with the man of your dreams, it'll taste like *haute cuisine*.

Decorating

If all this involves is a bit of painting then forget it. A bloke likes to feel a power tool in the palm of his hand. So, the more sanding, drilling and stripping involved, the better. You can either join in on the hard stuff or stand on the sidelines looking pathetic (therefore making him feel like he's doing a real man's job), depending on what breed of boy you've got. Either way, try to end up as filthy as possible therefore needing a bath together afterwards.

THINGS YOU'LL NEVER GET HIM TO DO
(WITHOUT A FIGHT)

1. Shopping for clothes (for him or you)
2. Going to the ballet
3. Rollerblading
4. Spending the weekend with the in-laws (also likely to end the relationship permanently).

On a more positive note:

THE MOST HIGHLY RECOMMENDED THINGS TO DO TOGETHER

1. Walking the dog
2. Weekly shop
3. Cycling
4. Going to the gym
5. Lying around doing nothing.

ACKNOWLEDGEMENTS

The publishers wish to thank the following for use of pictures:
Capital Pictures: 38, 39, 43, 64, 73
The Hulton Getty Picture Collection: 91
The Kobal Collection: 44, 45, 52, 56, 79
London Features International Ltd: 2
Rex Features Ltd: 24, 38, 60

Models
Lily Adams, Philip Auchinvole, Cristina Fagarazzi, Marcus Faithfull, Simon Holden, Janice Jones.